John the Baptist
Prophet and Evangelist

Carl R. Kazmierski

A Michael Glazier Book
THE LITURGICAL PRESS
Collegeville, Minnesota

Cover design by David Manahan, O.S.B. Ikon: St. John the Baptist, St. Catherine's Monastery, Sinai.

A Michael Glazier Book published by The Liturgical Press.

1   2   3   4   5   6   7   8   9

Library of Congress Cataloging-in-Publication Data

Kazmierski, Carl R.
   John the Baptist : prophet and evangelist / Carl R. Kazmierski.
      p.   cm.
   "A Michael Glazier book."
   Includes bibliographical references.
   ISBN 0-8146-5851-2
   1. John, the Baptist, Saint. I. Title.
BS2456.K388 1996
232.9'4—dc20   95-40742
                                                         CIP

Contents

Foreword

It is only with some hesitation that I offer these reflections on John the Baptist for publication. There is always so much more that can and perhaps must be written. I certainly do not consider these to be the "last words"—not even my own—on the topics that are addressed. Rather, my hope is that these words will be engaging enough to interest the reader in the person of John himself, in his movement, and in the challenges that we must face if we are to relate to one of the great figures in our collective history.

This is not an exhaustive or comprehensive study of the Baptist material in the New Testament. J. Ernst has published such an admirable work in 1989 (*Johannes der Täufer. Interpretation— Geschichte—Wirkungsgeschichte*. Berlin: Walter de Gruyter, 1989). Although it is not in English, it serves the scholarly community very well. I had no desire to duplicate his work, nor to produce a traditional academic study that would parallel his. Rather, I have attempted to approach some of the broader issues about the Baptist in New Testament interpretation and to reflect on them with the help of alternate patterns of interpretation, presenting them in a way that would be attractive to a broad spectrum of readers, both professional and lay. Nevertheless, I have taken pains to remain respectful of current exegetical practice, even when I have adopted new models to guide my exegesis.

Words of thanks and dedication are always difficult. There are some that cannot be expressed. While I should like to include so many for their support over the years, I choose two dear friends whose encouragement and support were responsible for my embarking on a path that has brought me much happiness and fulfillment. Both have since died, and it is to their memory that I dedicate this work.

Maurice Giroux, O.M.I.
Achille Ledent, O.M.I.
In memoriam

Introduction

In the last decade of the first century, the Jewish historian Flavius Josephus wrote a history of Judaism for his Roman protectors in which he recounts the disastrous rout of the army of Herod Antipas, who ruled Judea during the time of Jesus. "To some of the Jews," says Josephus, "the destruction of Herod's army seemed to be divine vengeance, and certainly a just vengeance, for his treatment of John, surnamed the Baptist" (*Antiquities* 18.5.2 no. 116). The text is important since it is the only contemporary reference to John that we have outside the New Testament. (It is not at all so clear, as is often supposed, that the references to John in the Gospel of Thomas 46 and 78 are independent of the Synoptics.) Actually Josephus is not that interested in the Baptist, and what he records is secondhand information at best. Nevertheless, what he has to say can help us to understand some of John's influence on the early Christians and round out the somewhat sketchy picture of the Baptist that even the most optimistic of historians might be able to draw from the Gospels.

Josephus further reports that many of the Jews had a high regard for John, which he seems, at least to some extent, to have shared. "Herod had him put to death," he continues, "though he was a good man and had exhorted the Jews to lead righteous lives, to practice justice towards their fellows and piety towards God, and so doing, to join in baptism" (*Antiquities* 18.5.2. no. 117). What caused the difficulty, moreover, was his extreme popularity and effectiveness. "When others too joined the crowds about him, because they were aroused to the highest degree by his sermons, Herod became alarmed . . . and decided that it would be much better to strike first and be rid of him before his work led to an uprising, than to wait for an upheaval, get involved in a difficult situation, and see his mistake'' (*Antiquities* 18.5.2 nos. 118–119).

This account of the reasons for Herod's execution of John does not seem to accord with that presented in the Gospels. But at the moment that is not our concern. For now it is important to note only two things; first, John is presented as having been an extremely popular preacher, and second, he was perceived to have been a threat to the one in authority. These two observations are important because, as we shall see, they will provide some insight into the development of the various traditions in the New Testament that are concerned with the Baptist.

Insignificant as Judea may have been to the larger world of the Roman Empire, one of its people, who is said to have referred to himself as ''a voice crying in the wilderness,'' was to set in motion a dynamic that was far more consequential than Herod could ever have imagined. The movement that he began was ultimately to shake the foundations of the Empire itself. The figure of John the Baptist stands at the beginning of Christian history, which for good or for bad was to preside over the Empire's dissolution and strangely enough, at the same time, to preserve its heritage for almost two thousand years. His was more than just an individual's struggle with God, as profound as that may be. It was the struggle of a people grappling with itself in such a way that it set a course of events that, even in this twentieth century, has not come to its fullness of time.

John proclaimed the Jewish ideal of the kingdom of God, and he himself soon became, within that tradition, the beginning of its Gospel, announcing not only the coming of the Christian Savior, but echoing its call for repentance and conversion across the centuries. Even today his is a voice in the wilderness, calling ever new generations to answer the challenge posed by his person so many centuries ago.

To hear that voice, however, may not be quite as easy as we sometimes suppose. In fact, we have to be very honest and admit that we know very little about the man himself. Yet who of us has not been influenced, perhaps even profoundly, by words which we barely heard, or persons we hardly knew? So too the early Christians were influenced by the figure of a man who stood out from among the crowds in their memory, by words that he spoke to their hearts in situations perhaps far different from those that he himself had envisioned. This is the stuff of life, the drama of our knowing, never fully, but nevertheless responding to what we glimpse of greatness and challenge.

John the Baptist appeared in the wilderness, wrapped in controversy from the very beginning. And it was a controversy that continued not only in his own time but in the generations that followed. Jesus is said to have considered him to be even greater than the prophets. He accepted baptism from him and even spent time as his disciple. Yet there were others who could not abide his coming. Perhaps it is here, then, in this world of discipleship and rejection, that we ought to begin our search for John—in the place of wilderness, in the place set apart and from which his voice was heard so long ago.

The fact that the traditions about John can be traced to every layer of the gospel tradition points to the early acceptance of a significant role for him in the life of the Church and in its understanding of its own mission. The Church could not ignore John, for his preaching nurtured the very roots of its own identity. Its traditions about him are therefore diverse and rich, each one reflecting a pattern of experience that goes beyond a first encounter.

From the beginning Christianity set John into the context of God's history (Mark 1:2-8), not as an isolated individual but as one who made a profound difference in the overall plan of God, that divine drama that the Bible proclaims. John was seen to be a part of that drama, the beginning of a new and decisive moment in the unfolding of the plot set out "in the beginning." In John it became news once again that God had entered into creation and had taken part in its history. John became a preacher of the gospel of God, an evangelist, one who, in word, work, and destiny began and foreshadowed the work of Jesus and the Church. Speaking with prophetic fervor, he appears on the horizon—on the edges of the world—in the desert places of civilized existence, in the areas of immediacy, religion, and faith.

The purpose of any work of this sort cannot be simply to study texts from a past age. Together we must try to make those texts come alive and speak to us so that we might understand and perhaps even be confronted by the mighty dynamic that underlies their very existence. We must seek to experience a solidarity with these people and their history; to hear their voices which reach out to us through the ages; to listen as they speak to each new generation that in turn brings with it its own life experience; to be drawn into conversation with the people who stand behind the texts, with the men and women who went before us and lived and loved much as we do; to wonder, and perhaps even to be blessed with new insight for our own journey.

For the believer this is the dynamic of the word of God. It is a word enshrined and forever set, but containing a power never exhausted, forever able to bid and draw those who take it up into dialogue, calling them to respond and perhaps even to Sabbath and contemplation.

Such is the voice of John the Baptist and that of Jesus who listened to him. Jesus became his follower and was to refer to him in the most challenging of terms. A generation later St. Mark was to present him as the first preacher of the gospel, to be followed by his redactors and matched, at the end of the first century, by the Fourth Evangelist, who was still struggling with his challenge to a community who now proclaimed Jesus as the Light of the World. Can this John still speak to the Church today in a way that would match the voice that cried out in the reign of Tiberius Caesar and spoke to the hearts of his adherents in the days of the Christian infancy?

Perhaps it is up to us to go aside for a while into our own desert place, to withdraw at least for a moment as did those who went out to see and to hear this "voice crying in the wilderness." Perhaps in our day we must make that same journey he called his first hearers to make in order to experience the Way to salvation, which only gradually unfolds in a world still seeking to know if indeed there is such a Way.

1

In the Shadows of the Kingdom

Beginning the Search

We begin our journey in search of John the Baptist in a place far distant from the shores of the Jordan River where he is said to have preached his message. For we are drawn to the Gospel of St. Luke, written toward the end of the first century, for a community as far removed from his desert experience as we are today. Luke is the only evangelist who gives us any information about the background and origins of John (Luke 1–2), and this is what we look for when we attempt to understand anything about a person. But the nature of Luke's narrative[1] makes it difficult to judge what he can really tell us. The traditions he uses, of course, serve as an introduction to the Third Gospel and present a kind of diptych in which the annunciation, birth, and naming of John serve as a parallel to the annunciation, birth, and naming of Jesus,[2] who, as Son of God, is the real center of the narrative. But the story is wonderful, and even if Luke uses the Baptist to set the stage for the even

---

[1] For literature on the opening chapters of St. Luke, see R. E. Brown, *The Birth of the Messiah* (Garden City: Doubleday, 1977) 253–255 and ibid., "Gospel Infancy Narrative Research from 1976 to 1986. Part II (Luke)," *Catholic Biblical Quarterly* 48 (1986) 660–680.

[2] For a full discussion of this, see J. Fitzmyer, *The Gospel According to St. Luke I* (Garden City: Doubleday, 1981) 313–321; R. Brown, *Birth of the Messiah*, 235–499, here especially 250–253.

more wonderful story of Jesus, we cannot be but struck by the reverence and awe with which the author presents him.

In their own right these traditions are worthy of serious study for their artistic and even lyrical quality. Many scholars feel that, at least in part, they have their origin in circles of the followers of John the Baptist and/or perhaps of early Christian Jews who had some connection with them.[3] While this would not remove the difficulties surrounding the interpretation of the texts within the Christian Gospel tradition, it does present the possibility that we might be able to detect a glimmer of an early pre-Gospel tradition about John that is not evidenced in other texts.

According to Luke, John was the son of the priest Zachary and his wife Elizabeth, who were kin to Mary, the mother of Jesus. Like Mary, Elizabeth is said to have been favored by God, and the son she was to bring forth, to be filled with the Holy Spirit (1:16). From all appearances the family seems not to have been of the Jerusalem circle of priests, but rather of the rural priesthood who would come to Jerusalem at set times to perform their Temple service,[4] spending the remainder of the year in the countryside, for the most part sharing the poverty and lifestyle of the peasant artisans and farmers.

In the announcement of the angel to Mary (1:15-17), Luke uses two images to describe John's mission, both of which appear in other forms in subsequent Baptist traditions. The first presents John as a Nazirite: "He will be great before the Lord," says the angel, "and he shall drink no wine nor strong drink, and he will be filled with the Holy Spirit, even from his mother's womb" (1:15 RSV). This image of John as a Nazirite[5] is picked up again in Luke 7:33, where Jesus refers to an accusation that had been made against the Baptist: "John came eating no bread and drinking no wine," he says, "and you say that he has a demon." The Lukan text is recognized as having been touched up by the evangelist in the light of the

[3] For example, see J. Fitzmyer, *Luke I* 316-317.

[4] See J. Jeremias, *Jerusalem in the Time of Jesus. An Investigation into Economic and Social Conditions during the New Testament Period*, trans. F. H. and C. H. Cave (London: S.C.M., 1969) 198-207.

[5] See *Interpreter's Dictionary of the Bible*, 3:526-527.

earlier allusions in 1:15.[6] Nevertheless, the text recognizes and specifies, in a unique manner, a Baptist tradition of withdrawal and ascetic rigor that is attested almost universally in the Gospel tradition.

In the second instance John is presented as being a prophet like Elijah: ''He will go before them in the spirit and power of Elijah, to turn the hearts of the fathers to the children, and the disobedient to the wisdom of the just, to make ready for the Lord a people prepared'' (v. 17 RSV), an allusion to Malachi 4:5-6. With this Elijah reference Luke introduces an image of interpretation that has a number of variations within the tradition and that is, by far and again, the most prominent and fruitful model used in the New Testament to interpret John. It is perhaps significant that Luke does not care to equate John with Elijah in this text, but is satisfied with a simple comparison: John is like Elijah. In the later references to John/Elijah, the comparison takes on a more pointed reference: John is Elijah come-back, but that is not necessarily the case here.[7] Does this text perhaps reflect an early interpretation of John among his own followers? This is the contention of J. Fitzmyer,[8] and it seems to have much going for it. Later we will examine this in detail and inquire into the origins and development of this image.

Aside from this we know nothing of the early life of John. The panel on the Baptist is closed with the beautiful portrait of his wondrous birth with the bestowal of his name and the notice that John ''was in the wilderness until the day of his manifestation'' (Luke 1:80 RSV). This last note is intriguing and has given impetus to a large body of literature studying the relation of the Baptist to the Qumran sectarians.[9] In the least it serves as an editorial preparation for the desert tradi-

---

[6] Fitzmyer, *Luke I*, 678, 680. See the parallel text in Matthew 11:18 = Q: ''John came neither eating nor drinking'' (RSV).

[7] The difficulties of a one-dimensional understanding of Luke's portrayal of the Baptist are discussed in R. J. Miller, ''Elijah, John and Jesus in the Gospel of Luke,'' *New Testament Studies* 34 (1988) 611–622.

[8] *Luke I*, 319–320.

[9] For bibliography and discussion see H. Braun, *Qumran und das Neue Testament* (Tübingen: J. C. B. Mohr [Paul Siebeck], 1966) 2:1–29.

tion that Luke will later include from Mark (1:4, parallel Luke 3:2) so that there may not be much here to fill out the curiosity of a historian, at least as far as John's early life is concerned. Having said as much, we will examine that possibility more carefully in chapter 2, on the chance that some common ground might be found between John and the Qumran faction that would shed light on the Baptist and his movement.

At this point, however, perhaps it would be good to review something of the world into which John was born. His was a world very different from twentieth-century America, yet it shows some of the same tensions and hopes that mark our own, albeit in a different guise. Such an examination might prove helpful then, not only in our understanding of the Baptist but also in our attempt at appropriating and responding to the dynamic of his word.

Israel and the Kingdom of God

It is not usual to set discussion of the Baptist within the context of Kingdom theology. But if in fact that was a major symbol of the hopes and aspirations of the Jewish community at his time,[10] to ignore it as the setting of his teaching is to indulge in a rigorism that has tended to divorce the study of the early Christian movement and its people from their very lifeblood. To speak of Israel and its God is to enter into a world of discourse, long not our own, where such associations were part and parcel with the participants' understanding of the ways of God with his people. Were we to overlook this, we would run the risk of painting a portrait that reflects our own image rather than that of John. To understand their words then, we must attempt to get behind the texts themselves to the dialogue that they reflect. This is no easy matter, for we enter from outside, and only at great risk.[11] We shall have to

---

[10] J. H. Charlesworth, "The Historical Jesus in Light of Writings Contemporaneous with Him," *ANRW* II 25.1, 451–476. See especially 463–469.

[11] The use of language and its extension (writing) is determined by culture. We cannot presume that our own culturally based understanding and use of words, forms, etc., was shared by the ancients. In fact, all the evidence is against this assumption.

tread lightly, therefore, as we attempt to discover the meaning that is encoded in the texts they have left us.[12]

Monotheism and the Doctrine of Creation

Hope for the advent or restoration of God's kingdom was rooted in the traditional Jewish belief in Yahweh as God of creation.[13] Developed and celebrated by Israel over more than a millennium of its history, it was in a sense a confession of faith in who they were,[14] the people of Yahweh who was Lord and ruler over all that was, creator and sustainer of the nation and of the cosmos itself. In its doctrine of creation, Israel was able to order its own experience with the world of the seen and the unseen and to present a coherent picture of the way things were. Outside of this reality there was but chaos, the "formless void and darkness" of Genesis 1. The powerful word of its ordering stood as the beginning of their own narrative history, enshrined as the teaching of Moses, who himself had stood in his presence and beheld God's "glory."[15] In this Torah, the people had come to know him as he had revealed his will for them through his servant and had promised to once again bless them with such a prophet (Deut 18:15).

Diverse, yet bound together by this common view of reality, the children of Abraham viewed the cosmos as reflecting a divine pattern, an ordering of reality in which all things had place. The main attribute of their God was holiness (Exod 3:2-6), and it was holiness that he demanded of his people (Lev

[12] In what follows I have attempted to benefit from the insights provided by cultural anthropology in my description of Israel and its value system, while at the same time avoiding the technical jargon and discussion that accompanies such endeavors. Rather than burden the text with footnotes, I shall provide occasional references to direct the reader to further studies.

[13] See R. Clifford, "The Hebrew Scriptures and the Theology of Creation," *Theological Studies* 46 (1985) 507–523.

[14] See the discussion in H. Mol, *Identity and the Sacred. A Sketch for a New Social-Scientific Theory of Religion* (Oxford: Blackwell, 1976), who uses as his point of departure the notion that "religion defines man and his place in the universe."

[15] Exodus 3:1-7; 33:17; 34:10, 29–35.

19:2). This holiness set Yahweh apart from all other gods and his people apart from all other peoples. Yet it was not this separateness in itself that was celebrated, but the singular "wholeness" that was its cause and its goal, for Yahweh alone was whole and complete unto himself, showing a complete harmony in his knowledge and will and in the effective power of his mighty word.[16] Such a vision sought salvation from the ever-threatening forces of chaos in the maintenance of the harmony and order that resided in God and that he had willed for his creation, the crowning glory of which was his own people. If it was believed that there was a place for everything, then it was God's will that everything be in its own place.[17] To be "in the image of God" (Gen 1:27 RSV) was to mirror that harmony. To achieve this was salvation, justice, and peace.

It was within this pattern of relations that the covenant was conceived and applied to all of creation, to society as well as to nature, and so to the families of Abraham who populated the land that had been set aside as their heritage among the nations. That Yahweh had created this order had been made manifest by his mighty acts of power on their behalf: He was God and King, his name to be blessed and extolled forever; it was his works which gave him thanks and his holy ones, praise, "speaking of the glory of his kingdom and telling aloud his power!" (Ps 145:11)

If in Torah Israel was understood to have "the Way" revealed by God and to find there the Law in which the will of God was made known, it then became incumbent upon her to take it to heart (Deut 6:4-7 RSV):

> Hear O Israel . . . these words which I command you this day shall be upon your heart; and you shall teach them diligently to your children, and shall talk of them when you sit in your house,

[16] For a description of a biblical three-zone model for describing God and Man, see B. J. Malina, *The New Testament World: Insights from Cultural Anthropology* (Atlanta: Knox, 1981) 60–67, here especially 64f.; B. DeGeradon, "L'homme en l'image de Dieu. Approche nouvelle à la lumière de l'anthropologie du sens commun," *Nouvelle Revue Théologique* 80 (1958) 683–695.

[17] B. J. Malina, *Christian Origins and Cultural Anthropology: Practical Models for Biblical Interpretation* (Atlanta: Knox, 1986) 20–27.

and when you walk by the way, and when you lie down, and when you rise.

This Torah called for affirmation and response. It called for humble obedience by king and peasant alike, an obedience that affirmed the supremacy of God and the splendor of God's creation:

> The Lord our God is one Lord;
> and you shall love the Lord your God with all your heart,
> and with all your soul, and with all your might. (RSV)

This was the highpoint of wisdom: the fear of God, a reverent awe that not only saw God as God but as well recognized and accepted Israel as God's people, whose fulfillment was to be found in that very fact of dependence. To accept God as God was to accept the limitations of their own humanity that that implied. To effectively accomplish that was to achieve the goal of life, *Shalom*, the peace of God, which was for Israel the ultimate gift of the creator for his creatures.[18]

Preserving the Order of Creation

The ordering of society in Israel took on a kind of military precision since, from the beginning, Yahweh was seen as a divine warrior, the leader of the people in the face of the overwhelming forces of evil. "Who is like you, O Lord, among the gods," they prayed in one of the earliest songs of their tradition,

> Who is like you, majestic in holiness;
> terrible in glorious deeds, doing works of wonder?

> You stretched out your right hand,
> and the earth swallowed them!

> In your mercy you have been a leader to the people that you have redeemed;

[18] In sociocultural terms this would represent the "Core-Value" of Jewish society. See Malina, *Christian Origins*, 112–115.

and in your strength you have carried them to your holy dwelling
place. . . .

Yahweh will reign forever and ever! (Exod 15:11-13, 18).

The reign of this God was to be manifest both in the immediate concerns of the children of Abraham that affected their
day-to-day existence, as well as in the larger concerns of the
people in their necessary dealings with those outside. Covenant with God was to mark both family[19] and nation[20] as each
struggled to understand and abide by the divinely set parameters of social intercourse. Thus came the rules of purity, of
"clean" and "unclean." Who were the members of this
people? How were they to maintain themselves in the grace
of that election? Over the centuries an elaborate system was
developed to assure Israel that it could indeed answer those
questions.[21] In a society that placed such high stakes on be-
longing, there was no room for the type of identity crisis that
so often marks our own.

What this means, of course, is that the patterns of relationship that developed in both kinship and political systems
tended, once they were adopted, to remain in place. Instruction in the "Way of the Lord," Torah became Sacred Text; its
interpretation, the "traditions of the elders" against which
all else was measured. Being true to this tradition was the
surest/only way to achieve the goals of society and the life that
it supported. The most powerful people in that society, therefore, were the interpreters of the tradition. Kings and priests,
prophets and wise men became the arbiters of the nation's life
in good times and in bad. Thus the question of legitimacy in
each of these roles was forever posed and underlies a great
deal of the tension that marks Israel's life in the first century
as well. Who is the legitimate king, priest, prophet, or wise
man? Was it the one who sat in the chair of authority, or was

---

[19] Genesis 12:1-3; 15; 17.

[20] 2 Samuel 7:14-16; Psalm 2:7; 72; 110; 145.

[21] M. Douglas, *Purity and Danger: An Analysis of Concepts of Taboo* (London: Routledge and Kegan Paul, 1966). For a clear and succinct description of the first-century Jewish purity system, see B. Malina, *The New
Testament World*, 122–152.

it perhaps another to be sent by God? "Are you 'The One Who Is to Come,' or shall we look for another?" (Matt 11:3). Such was the question John sent his disciples to ask of Jesus. The answer to such questions was not always so obvious in first-century Israel! But their importance should not be doubted.

Kingdom Failure and the Rise of Messianism

By the time of John, of course, this process had been tested and honed by a system that had undergone many successes, but as many failures as well. In the sixth century the prophet Jeremiah had already bewailed the fate of Israel and the destruction of its life as being the result of its own abandonment of the covenant ideals. The deuteronomic history of its kings as well had become a scathing judgment on its perceived lack of fidelity. With the subsequent failure of the restoration and the move toward accommodation that gained momentum during the Hellenistic period, the prophetic promise that Yahweh would exercise his rule through his anointed one took on a confident urgency that gave birth to various movements that were to present an idealized vision of the nation and of its anointed leaders.[22] Such idealization functioned in the realm of national life and gave rise to ideologies that were basically political. To speak of a Messiah, whether of David or of Aaron, was to make an essentially political statement that could have profound consequences for the stance one was to take in contemporary society. It was to propose that traditional values could not be realized, and that, for whatever reason, the system had failed and needed to be repaired. There was a need for salvation from the forces of chaos that once more threatened the order that God had willed.[23]

---

[22] See now the discussion in R. A. Horsley and J. Hanson, *Bandits, Prophets and Messiahs: Popular Movements in the Time of Jesus* (Minneapolis: Winston, 1985); J. Neusner, et al., eds., *Judaisms and Their Messiahs at the Turn of the Christian Era* (Cambridge: Cambridge University, 1987).

[23] There seems never to have been a time in the history of Israel when such tension did not exist in one form or another. Indeed some would argue that conflict is inherent in the nature of society itself. It is, therefore, not at all clear that one can understand first-century Roman Pales-

Such salvation was indeed assured, for Yahweh was Lord, even though for the moment he may seem to have withdrawn his face from Israel. Once again he would set up his anointed on the throne of David and restore the priesthood to its rightful state of purity. Had he not said of David, "I will establish the throne of his kingdom forever," and promised, "I shall be his father, and he shall be my son?" (2 Sam 7:13-14 RSV). Had not the priesthood again and again repeated the holy words of anointing, "I will tell of the decree of the Lord: He said to me, 'You are my son, today I have begotten you' " (Ps 2:7 RSV).

In a remarkable fashion Israel was able to read the signs of its times and to enshrine even in its prayer a hard sense of realism,

> . . . now you have cast off and rejected,
> you are full of wrath against your anointed.
> . . . you have defiled his crown in the dust (Ps 89:38-39 RSV).

Yet Yahweh had promised,

> I will not remove from him my steadfast love,
> or be false to my faithfulness.
> I will not violate my covenant . . .
> his throne . . .
> . . . shall stand firm while the skies endure (vv. 35–37 RSV).

It remained now only to wait the arrival of the fullness of his time when he would make "the nations (their) heritage, and the ends of the earth (their) possession" (Ps 2:8 RSV).

In the meantime the zealous made accommodation based, for the most part, on their status in or relationship to one or another of the basic institutions of society.[24] The political an-

---

tine as a land where oppression and profound alienation pit one class against the other, as has been common in recent studies of the background of the Jesus movement. We shall discuss this later. We must be careful not to presume that the conditions (social and economic structures) for Marxist analysis were present in first-century Roman Palestine!

[24] As already inferred, there were but two separate social "institutions" in first-century Mediterranian society, namely, kinship and politics. All

swer in its most radical form was exemplified in the Essene movement with their covenant community of priests at Qumran on the shores of the Dead Sea. Other messianic movements, such as those headed by the prophet Theudas,[25] were more ad hoc and temporary political reactive movements among the peasants that lacked the cohesiveness and structure afforded by the "Lawyers" at Qumran.[26] On the other hand, movements with fictive structures based within the kinship system provided perhaps the most stable and easily accessible forms of accommodation within peasant society. Their function, while not directly "political," could indeed have a political impact, as did the Pharisee movement at the time of Salome Alexandra (76–67 B.C.).[27] At any rate, the existence of these various groups manifests that a number of avenues of protest were open for those who were not able to access the promised goals that society had at least theoretically set for itself under the aegis of its Lord, Yahweh, the God Most High.

Perhaps the most telling evidence of this is preserved in the synagogue prayer that may have served as part of the background for the prayer that Jesus was to teach his own disciples:

> Magnified and sanctified be his great name in the world that he has created according to his will; May he establish his kingdom in your lifetime and in your days, and in the lifetime of all the house of Israel, even speedily and at a near time.[28]

---

others, such as economics, education, and religion, were intricately bound up in these, so that they can not be understood as separate entities. For example, the "religion of Israel" inheres in both political and family institutions and cannot be described aside from either. To provide such a description would necessarily be anachronistic. See B. Malina, "Religion in the World of Paul," *Biblical Theology Bulletin* 16 (1986) 92–101.

[25] Josephus, *Antiquities* 20:97–98.

[26] See R. A. Horsley, " 'Like One of the Prophets of Old': Two Types of Popular Prophets at the Time of Jesus," *Catholic Biblical Quarterly* 47 (1985) 435–463.

[27] T. A. Burkhill, "Sanhedrin," *Interpreter's Dictionary of the Bible* 4:215.

[28] See Norman Perrin, *Rediscovering the Teaching of Jesus* (New York and Evanston: Harper and Row, 1967) 57. For the original Aramaic text see G. Dalman, *Die Worte Jesu*, I (Darmstadt: Wissenschaftliche Buchgesellschaft, 1965; reprint of the 2nd edition Leipzig, 1930) 82 and note 2.

Kingdom expectation indeed ran high in first-century Palestine, but ideas of what it actually entailed were as varied as the groups that adopted that imagery to articulate their deepest trust and hope in the power of their God.

Summary

As we attempt to understand the message of John the Baptist, and perhaps to appropriate it for our own journey, our first steps lead us into a world very different from our own. John's preaching of the kingdom was rooted in his people's understanding of their own existence and of their place in the order of God's creation. It was Yahweh who called Israel to holiness and provided them with the means to achieve that wholeness which would bring his creation to its fullness. If in fact such was not yet the case, then the assurance was there that soon the promised fulfillment would be upon them. In the meantime, however, alternate interpretations of Torah would provide accommodation to those who would await its coming in the age of the Messiah.

2

Water in the Wilderness

Ad Modum Recipientis

From all appearances John does not follow in the footsteps of his father, for the first we hear of him after the solemn presentation by Luke in the introduction to his work is of his sudden appearance in the desert places of the Jordan Valley, practicing what is described as a "baptism of repentance for the forgiveness of sins." The tradition is unanimous in this; John was a desert preacher. That should startle us. For if Luke is correct about John's background, a shocking thing has taken place. If his father Zachary was a priest, and there is no reason to deny this,[1] then John's destiny likewise lay in the priesthood. To abandon this role would be unheard of in the society of his time.[2] Yet this seems to have been the case.

The adoption of such a singular lifestyle for the son of a priest, then, posed questions to his contemporaries that would have to be faced squarely. The issues involved were far too serious to simply be ignored. Had John been a "loner" and not attracted the following that he had, he could perhaps have

[1] See C. Kraeling, *John the Baptist* (New York: Scribner's, 1951) 28; J. Ernst, *Johannes der Täufer, Interpretation—Geschichte—Wirkungsgeschichte* (Berlin: Walter de Gruyter, 1989) 269–272.

[2] B. J. Malina, *The New Testament World*, 51–60, and ibid., "The Individual and the Community—Personality in the Social World of Early Christianity," *Biblical Theology Bulletin* 9 (1979) 126–138.

been written off as "beside himself,"[3] and that would have been it. But "all the country of Judea and all the people of Jerusalem went out to him," says Mark (1:5), and even given the hyperbole of the evangelist, Josephus confirms that the crowds were great indeed (*Antiquities* 18.5.2 no. 118). In a culture whose structures were rooted in the principle of "a place for everyone and everyone in his place," John posed a challenge. His contemporaries could not but react!

It is an old maxim that "actions speak louder than words." Why was John acting in the way that he was? What was it about him that seemed to strike such a chord of recognition, challenge, and response? For his contemporaries his being in the wilderness was as important as what he had to say. Perhaps even more so, for it called for interpretation and judgment. Often one's deeds are perceived quite differently from the way they are intended. Sometimes that is because in themselves they are ambiguous and have not been clearly explained. In that case the fault lies with the "speaker." But at other times the fault may lie in the "eyes of the beholder." Some contemporary critics speak of a plurality of meanings as being inherent in texts because of those elements of "meaning" that are brought to their interpretation by their readers. The Scholastics expressed something of the same insight in a maxim that is helpful here: *"Quidquid recipitur,"* they would say, *"ad modum recipientis recipitur."*[4] In other words, people comprehend things according to their own capacity. We should understand this to refer to a broad cultural capacity shaped by the world of one's experience and the patterns of interpretation of that experience that are generally accepted by one's contemporaries.[5]

---

[3] It was such rumor that, according to Mark 3:21, caused Jesus' family to have concern for him. See M. Zerwick, *Biblical Greek* (Rome: PIB, 1964) 2 (no. 4) for *elegon* in this verse as an "indefinite plural."

[4] F. Annen (*Heil für die Heiden. Zur Bedeutung und Geschichte der Tradition vom besessenen Gerasener* [*Mk 5,1-20 parr.*] (Frankfurt am Main: Josef Knecht, 1976), explicitly adopts this principle in his interesting attempt to develop a contemporary specter for interpretation.

[5] For a discussion of sociolinguistic theory, see especially E. Leach, *Culture and Communication: The Logic by Which Symbols are Connected* (Cambridge: Cambridge University Press, 1976); M.A.K. Halliday, *Language*

Even in the New Testament John has been interpreted in different ways. While for the most part these interpretations may not contradict each other, at times they do. Was John Elijah, or not? It's one of those questions that you have to answer by saying "that depends on whom you talk to." In Matthew and Mark there is no question about it, "John is Elijah" (Mark 9:11 parallel Matt 17:12; Matt 11:14). One may discuss whether or not Luke is comfortable with that understanding of the Baptist,[6] but there can be no question that the Gospel of John denies it outright (1:21)![7] If there is such room for diversity of interpretation among those who shared so much with him, how much more likely is it that we would be able to understand John as he intended, separated as we are by such a great distance of culture, time, and place. How indeed would John like to have been understood? Is it necessary to pursue such investigations, when, as is often argued, all we seek is found in faith? Is it useful? Is it even possible to know, or are we to be satisfied with only "an echo of his whisper" as J. Reumann has suggested?[8]

The Qumran Connection

Many scholars have suggested that John spent some time in his youth with the Essenes, a cohesive Jewish movement,[9] which appears to have had a settlement near the shores of the

---

as *Social Semiotic: The Social Interpretation of Language and Meaning* (Baltimore: University Park, 1978) and its application to biblical interpretation by B. Malina, *Christian Origins and Cultural Anthropology: Practical Models for Biblical Interpretation* (Atlanta: Knox, 1986) especially 1–27.

[6] See J. Fitzmyer, "The Lucan Picture of John the Baptist as Precursor of the Lord," in ibid., *Luke the Theologian: Aspects of His Teaching* (New York/Mahwah: Paulist, 1989) 86–116; R. J. Miller, "Elijah, John and Jesus in the Gospel of Luke," *New Testament Studies* 34 (1988) 611–622.

[7] See R. Brown, *The Gospel According to John I*, 47–49.

[8] "The Quest for the Historical Baptist," *Understanding the Sacred Text* J. Reumann, ed. (Valley Forge: Judson, 1972) 187.

[9] It is possible to argue that too much stress has been placed on the dissident stance of the Essene group, an emphasis that has often led to a far too one-sided picture of the movement as the radical opposition, even in the time of Jesus.

Dead Sea at Qumran, not far from Jerusalem. According to John 3:23 (RSV), he baptizes at "Aenon, near Salim," which some commentators place not far from what seems to have been these community headquarters.[10] Furthermore, there appear to be some striking parallels between his own preaching and practice of baptism and the traditions of that community. If we could establish that John was a member of that community, we might be able to place him within a clearer and more specific context, which would help us to answer some of the questions that we have just posed. Since the discovery of the Dead Sea Scrolls in 1947, scholars have put together a remarkably detailed picture of the Qumran group, which is said to have been one of the most influential of his time.

According to this view, the Essenes originally seem to have been a group of dissident priests, a faction which separated from the Jerusalem leadership because of disagreement about the legitimacy of the incumbent high priest and even perhaps of the "rubrics" of the Temple and its sacrifices.[11] From their own testimony we know that they[12] went out into the desert to seek and indeed to await the coming of the Lord:

> Now when these things happen to the community in Israel, they will separate from the perverse men who dwell there according to these directions, and go to the wilderness, there to clear the way of the Lord, as it is written, 'In the wilderness clear the way of the Lord; level in the desert a highway for our God' (1QS 8:12-16).

[10] In fact, such a location is not probable. See R. Brown, *The Gospel According to John I*, 151.

[11] See D. J. Harrington, *The Maccabean Revolt: Anatomy of a Biblical Revolution* (Wilmington: Glazier, 1988) 119–123. For an introduction to the Qumran discoveries and their interpretation, F. M. Cross, *The Ancient Library of Qumran and Modern Biblical Studies*, revised edition (New York: Doubleday, 1961) is still the classic work (reprint ed.: Grand Rapids: Baker Book House, 1980).

[12] Were the inhabitants of the fortress at Qumran really Essenes as has been generally accepted? For a dissenting view worthy of serious consideration, see N. Golb, "The Problem of Origin and Identification of the Dead See Scrolls," *Proceedings of the American Philosophical Society*, 124 (1980) 1–24; ibid., "Who Hid the Dead Sea Scrolls?" *Biblical Archaeologist* 48 (1985) 68–82.

Of course, the text that they call on for justification of their desert sojourn[13] is Isaiah 40:3, the same text that the Gospels use to describe the ministry of John. In fact, the Fourth Evangelist, in the wonderful passage in which the Baptist gives testimony to Jesus, has John himself answer the priests and Levites sent by the Temple authorities in the strains of that same poem from Isaiah:

> I am the voice of one crying in the wilderness.
> "Make straight the way of the Lord!" (RSV).

Was John then a member of this Qumran group? It is not impossible. As we have seen, Luke's remark that the child "stayed in the desert until the day of his public appearance to Israel" (Luke 1:80) has been taken by some as a strong hint that this was so.[14] Josephus tells us that the Essenes had the practice of adopting children in order to train them in their "way of righteousness."[15] If his parents were of advanced age, as Luke tells us, then, it is argued, there would be every possibility that John was given over to this community at their death.[16] Surely this would fill in the lost years of John before he is said to have appeared so abruptly in the wilderness, coming in the "way of righteousness." It would also provide some background for the peculiarity of his baptismal ritual, connected as it is with the "forgiveness of sins" (1QS 5:13-14).[17]

Yet the parallels are not exact. Mediterranean cultural practice would militate against any such practice of childrearing by celibate men, as are supposed to have populated Qumran. So too, Luke certainly gives us no hint that John's family shared the legendary opposition of Qumran to the Jerusalem priest-

---

[13] J.A.T. Robinson ("The Baptism of John and the Qumran Community: Testing a Hypothesis," *Harvard Theological Review* 50 [1957] 175–191, here especially 178–179) interprets this text, wrongly, I think, in a radically futurist-eschatological sense.

[14] See especially Robinson, "Baptism."

[15] Robinson, 185; Josephus, *War* 2.120; 1QSa 1, 4–18.

[16] Robinson, 176.

[17] See Robinson, 180–184, and J. Fitzmyer, "The Lucan Picture," 93–94 for a discussion of the difficulties associating this practice with proselyte baptism.

hood,[18] and any such decision would have been a family affair, to say the least. On the contrary, the peasant priesthood was more likely to seek respite from any tension with the Jerusalem hierarchy in an altogether different pattern of response than that developed at Qumran, whose roots were among the elite of society themselves.[19] Furthermore, there is not even a hint in the tradition that John's movement was in any way structured, as was that of Qumran, who in essence merely replaced the accepted structures of the Jerusalem elite with their own, which were modeled on an idealization of the Jerusalem pattern. What the Essenes provided was an idealized state, peopled by the holy remnant, the elect few who were ready to replace the one that, in their belief, was soon to be overthrown by an angry deity,[20] for it had brought pollution to the Holy City. While they had in fact lost any position of honor they may have had in society, they were able to maintain and even increase their "honor-rating" by creating a new context for it among themselves.

John, on the other hand, seems to have called out to all of Israel and to have challenged both elite and peasant alike to

[18] P. Hollenbach, "Social Aspects of John the Baptizer's Preaching Mission in the Context of Palestinian Judaism," in *ANRW* II.19.1 (1979) 850–875, stresses the "profound alienation" from the elite Jerusalem priestly families suffered by the rural priesthood as the background for his discussion of John's ministry. In our opinion Hollenbach tends to greatly overstate his case. See also J. Ernst, *Johannes der Täufer*, 271: "a twentieth century legend."

[19] Cross, *Ancient Library*, 129. It is difficult to understand how Hollenbach ("Social Aspects," 853) can call on Cross to support his characterization of Qumran as "a monastic group that consisted largely of lower rural priests." In fact, Cross states just the opposite.

[20] Whether the longing that was expressed in apocalyptic imagery was always matched by an expectation of its imminent fulfillment is a question that is beginning to pose itself. See J. J. Collins, "The Apocalyptic Technique: Setting and Function in the Book of Watchers," *Catholic Biblical Quarterly* 44 (1982) 91–111, here especially 109–111, and ibid., *The Apocalyptic Imagination: An Introduction to the Jewish Matrix of Christianity* (New York: Crossroad, 1984). In reference to Qumran, see especially 113–141.

accept his baptism.[21] And if there is any truth at all to Matthew's characterization of Pharisees and Sadducees among those who submitted to him,[22] then, despite the scathing rebuff that the tradition hurls at them as a group,[23] their presence at the waters of the Jordan cannot be dismissed. Are we to presume that there was no "Nicodemus" among them at all? Even Jeremiah found support among the councils of the mighty (Jer 26:16-24)! The Baptist's movement, therefore, was more of a threat than that of Qumran, for it was capable of building a more widely based faction that could have serious political repercussions for all involved. According to Josephus, this is exactly what Herod perceived (*Antiquities* 18.5.2 no. 118).

One must tread lightly therefore, and perhaps look to a milieu that provided a pattern of reaction and response to a situation far different from those that were at the root of Qumran's experience. While there may be some parallels between his own practices and those of Qumran, it is perhaps more likely that his lifestyle and preaching were the result of his own unique insight, building on the same values that would have influenced the Essenes and others in his generation, but not on any direct connection with that group itself.[24] By the time of John the Qumran influence was certainly diffused throughout Judaism. Their movement had existed for almost two hundred years. Many of its characteristics were shared by other

[21] In contrast to Hollenbach, "Social Aspects," it is not possible to assign specific audiences to the various sayings attributed to John. Most of these are clearly redactional and even in some cases contradictory, so that one must be extremely careful not to force them into any preconceived patterns as he is tempted to do.

[22] The audience provided by Matthew for the saying of the Baptist (3:7-10, parallel Luke 3:7-9) is most clearly redactional, but that does not mean to say that it can be dismissed as a fiction of the evangelist. See Kazmierski, "Stones," 27-29.

[23] For the argument that this condemnation of Pharisees and Sadducees is to be found not in the ministry of John but in that of the early Christian mission, see Kazmierski, op. cit.; below, chapter 6.

[24] Throughout his article Robinson is too eager to make connections between John and Qumran, as his almost breathless discovery of so many "possibilities" suggests!

groups as well.[25] It is clear that one of these was a common pool of images and texts that were used in the search for legitimacy in a time of ambiguity and doubt.

Yet how can we measure the influences in a person's life that cause him to take one path rather than another? It would be foolish to rule out any possibility when we have so little to go on. Certainly the raw material was there, at hand for a creative soul to mold into something new. Such is the genius of the prophetic figure, the quality which would establish his status and allow for the kind of reputation that seems to have followed upon the work of John. Why else the crowds? Why the opposition, if not because what he had to say was marked by that glimmer of new insight that gives form and shape to a new word waiting to be heard?

A Voice in the Desert

For all our justified skepticism about the "Qumran connection," it is likely, therefore, that the use of the prophecies of the Second Isaiah to describe the Baptist's work, is indeed the bedrock of that tradition. It is interesting to note that the Gospels have used another version of the text of Isaiah than that found at Qumran. Or perhaps they have adapted the text in order to highlight their own application of it to a new time and place. As introduced by St. Mark, the text is not simply a quotation from Isaiah but a composite in which two or three similar prophetic texts are combined. Mark does indeed cite the (accommodated) Isaiah text: "The voice of one crying in the wilderness: prepare the way of the Lord, make straight his paths" and in this is followed by both Matthew and Luke who quote exactly the same form of the text. Mark means to describe the appearance of the Baptist as the preparation and indeed the beginning of the proclamation of the Gospel that he himself is setting out to preach. The beginning of the (preaching) of the Gospel of and about Jesus the Christ and Son of God is in accord with Isaiah.[26] Consequently it is "according

[25] For a full discussion, see Horsley, *Bandits*.
[26] See C. R. Kazmierski, *Jesus, the Son of God: A Study of the Markan Tradition and its Redaction by the Evangelist* (Würzburg: Echter, 1979) 2–26.

to Isaiah . . ." that John appears in the wilderness. But Mark, and Mark alone, proceeds to add a further citation[27] that is adjusted[28] to heighten his own Christological application of that text:

> Behold,
> I will send my messenger before your face
> who will prepare your way.

This is one of those places where abandoning the theory of Markan priority would make our task a great deal easier,[29] but there are simply too many cautions against accepting that as a solution to Synoptic difficulties. At any rate it is interesting that the Isaianic model is used to describe the Baptist only here in the Synoptics, and that, at least in Mark, it is already reinterpreted by the use of another text with its implicit connection to the prophet Elijah.[30] Perhaps even more important is the fact, often overlooked, that the explicit reference to Isaiah is actually directed beyond the Baptist to Jesus and his ministry. The point that Mark is making is that because John has fulfilled this prophecy of Isaiah, by appearing as a desert

[27] In the perspective of the two-source hypothesis, both Matthew and Luke would have omitted the reference to Malachi that they found in Mark, Matthew only to use it in Jesus' description of John in 11:10 of his Gospel, (where it was already in his Q source?) and Luke in the parallel text to Matthew in 7:27. The evangelist Mark would have either created the composite himself or adopted what was already a composite text in the tradition and used it to signal his understanding of the work of the Baptist in reference to Jesus: To prepare the way of the Lord (Jesus). Matthew and Luke would have then separately omitted the reference to Malachi 3:1 because (1) they recognized it for what it was (not from Isaiah); (2) they found the reference to Malachi in the story of Jesus' teaching about the Baptist in their common source and wished to use it within that context (Elijah reference).

[28] This is often described as a conflation of Malachi 3:1 with Exodus 23:30. We will discuss this more fully in chapter 5.

[29] The major objection to the two-source theory is still the problem presented by the so-called minor agreements in the triple tradition of Matthew and Luke as over against Mark, of which this would seem to be a striking example.

[30] Malachi 3:23.

preacher, Jesus' ministry receives legitimation. It is the scriptural argument par excellence that calls for the reader's recognition that Jesus has divine authority for doing what he does. What else is necessary! It is furthermore clearly confirmed by the proclamation of the heavenly voice, which accompanies his anointing as Isaianic Servant of God at his baptism by John and reveals him as such to his disciples on the Mount of Transfiguration.

So John is able, in this tradition, to become a means of legitimation for the proclamation of the Church, a development which does not reach its fullness until the Fourth Gospel. But that is a development that we will examine later. Our immediate concern is the root of this development in the model of the Isaianic evangelist. John is "a voice crying in the wilderness." So too were the covenenters of Qumran. The presence of such a pattern of interpretation would enable the Christian Church to develop its own presentation of John and account for the difficulties it faced in its remembrance of his relation with their Master, who had been his disciple. Was it not also available to John himself and to his own followers?

"The voice of one crying in the wilderness!" Such a simple claim perhaps even belabors the obvious and therefore cannot claim any exclusive ownership within the Qumran tradition, or, for that matter, in the supposed Christian manipulation of the Baptist material. What could be more natural for a man of John's striking singularity than to explain his strange bearing and practice by pointing to a prophetic text that was ready at hand? The text had come to serve as a kind of cipher, a prophecy which had been used to initiate a desert experience as the preparation for God's intervention in the lives of his people. It was now to become the driving force of a movement whose influence would certainly touch them all.

The Social Aspect of Desert Theology

As we have seen, the Fourth Gospel confirms that this was the Baptist's own explanation of his mission (John 1:23). If, as we have argued, this is in fact so, then it is against this prophetic background that he would have his audience meet him in the desert places, on the fringes of society. But much as the prophets of old had done in the past, John preached a message that was a two-edged sword. Indeed, such challenges had been posed before. But time and again "their ears were dull and their eyes closed" so that it could not enter into their hearts and bring them to conversion (Isa 6:10-11; Mark 4:10-11).

"Hear this, you foolish and senseless people," said the prophet Jeremiah,

> You who have eyes but see not,
> who have ears but hear not . . .
> this people has a stubborn and rebellious heart;
> they have turned aside and gone away. . . .
> They do not say in their hearts,
> 'Let us fear the Lord our God' (5:21, 23, 24 RSV).

The Gospels tell us that one day Jesus posed such a challenge to the crowds who were surrounding him: "What did you go out in the desert to see?" (Matt 11:7). What indeed! A rather stark figure, who, from all reports, had broken the boundaries of accepted behavior for a child of Abraham. Jesus' question was not an idle one, for it would give him some insight into their response to what he himself had to say. After all, he had been closely associated with John. As he asserts, the question could be answered in a number of different ways. It depended on what kind of associations his hearers had brought to their experience of John's word. He poses the same question to the Pharisees who try to trap him. "Tell me," he says, "was the baptism of John from heaven or from men?" (Mark 11:30). And they refuse to answer.

The question is posed time and again in the Gospels. It is a question that, in one sense, summarizes the inherent ambiguity of a person's actions. What gives meaning to the things we do? In our generation we would probably ask, "What did you intend to prove?" In the first century this question would have been posed in terms of authority and personal causality. "By whose authority does he do these things?" What right had John to speak the text of the desert? Who empowered him to do what he was doing? Since it obviously was not someone in the world of the seen, it must be someone in that of the unseen. The process here is one of the "discernment of spirits."[31] This was the question that now imposed itself about John.

John's actions, then, were signs that needed to be read. The range of possible readings, however, was rather narrow. In fact, there were only two. It was either because he was possessed by the Spirit of God or by the Spirit of Satan. If it was by the Spirit of God that John did what he was doing, then he was a prophet and should be revered and obeyed. If, on the other hand, it was because he was possessed by the Spirit of Beelzebul, the prince of demons, then he was a witch and must be segregated and removed from society because he could bring only evil and curse.[32] We do the same thing in our own society, albeit with different labels, but with social consequences that are sometimes devastating to the ones involved and always damaging to the integrity of the community.[33]

Two realities stand out in the desert tradition in Israel, reflecting in a way not only the two possible interpretations of John, but the two poles of social integration within the community as well. On the one hand the desert was remembered as a place of temptation and failure. It was pictured as the dwelling place of unclean spirits and demons who not only corrupt but symbolize all the evil and pollution that threaten the wholeness and holiness of the people. It was against these that the boundaries of the Law had set Israel, demanding ever-present vigilance were she to maintain the purity demanded to serve in the House of the All Holy One. For those elements of society where there was a high degree of match between expectations and experience, the desert would symbolize the place "outside the camp." To live there was to ignore the boundaries

---

[31] Jesus' activity presented his contemporaries with the same challenge. See Mark 3:21-30; below, chapter 3.

[32] See Mary Douglas, *Purity and Danger;* and ibid., *Natural Symbols: Explorations in Cosmology* (London: Penguin, 1973).

[33] Labeling theory within the sociology of deviance provides a very fruitful model for understanding the process that ensues. See E. Pfuhl, *The Deviance Process* (New York: Van Nostrand, 1980) and C. Kazmierski, "Stones," 35-38.

of civilization, to act with a certain air of defiance and risk bringing pollution upon oneself and the community as well. Was
that the case with John? Was he a man possessed by the spirit
of uncleanness? Such was the charge that Jesus relates was
indeed brought against him.

Life was funny. Jesus came "eating and drinking" and was
accused by his opponents of being a glutton and a drunkard.
John was just the opposite. They should have been satisfied
that he was a holy man. "John came among you neither eating nor drinking and you say, 'he has a demon.'" What was
one to do? Indeed, what was John and those who were among
his disciples to do? For they were met with an opposition that
was far more dangerous than would appear to the eye. An
accusation of "having a demon" was a charge as serious as
any that could be made; its purpose, the ultimate banishment
of the person from society itself, its perpetrators, those whose
vision of society or their place within it was publicly questioned
by this strange preacher. "John has a demon" means that
the spirit that is within him is the spirit of uncleanness that
brings pollution upon the holy land and marks him as one who
is not fit to stand among the people of God. It is a charge of
desperation that could be uttered by both Sadducee and
Pharisee alike, and for that matter, by any of the rivaling groups
in the land of promise.

Indeed, John was set aside by his lifestyle on the fringe of
society, amidst the home of demons and robbers. He fasts. He
has no wife. He wears the garments of a madman! John's
presence in the desert is a disturbing one for many because
it intimates quite clearly that God cannot be found in their
midst. Israel is not the community that she ought be, for otherwise there would be no need for a holy man to withdraw and
make such a call to repentance. From this perspective John's
call is indeed a pronouncement of judgment, perhaps a prophetic curse. He seems to hit at all the organized Torah groups
who must indeed respond if they are to maintain their status[34]

---

[34] For the role which "honor" played in first-century Mediterranean
society, see B. Malina, *The New Testament World*, 25–50. Even though the
various Torah-groups *(Haberim)* cannot be considered to have been of the
elite of society (high-grid in the Douglas-Malina scattergram [see B. Malina,

as legitimate options for fulfilling the ideal of Israel. But their response takes the form of an accusation that will needs have a far-reaching effect for all those involved. Their accusations, in fact, are an attempt at exercising social control in a situation that is ambiguous at least, if not threatening and perhaps even inflammatory. The question was one of honor and legitimacy, which struck at the core of their self-understanding. The result of such a response is that a dynamic of challenge and riposte is set up that must continue to the end if the subject and those who have gathered around him are to maintain any semblance of honor and respect.

The evangelist Mark narrates a scene in which Jesus was later to face the same charge and answers it with a scathing rebuke that resounds to this day and sends shivers up and down the spine: "Whoever blasphemes against the Holy Spirit never has forgiveness, but is guilty of an eternal sin" (3:29, see 21-30 RSV). Jesus' opponents were not able to discern by which spirit Jesus was filled! In our time we might be tempted to view this simply as a question of human motivation, but who is to say that the ancients were so wrong in their seeking of outside agents for human actions?

There is another side to the story, however. Jesus had accepted baptism at the hands of John. So too had so many others. John's Gospel tells us of Peter and Andrew, who were later to be disciples of Jesus (1:35-43), while Matthew (11:2-6, parallel Luke 7:18-23) tells us of John's disciples who came to Jesus as messengers of the Baptist. The most important point that the historian Josephus wants to tell us about John is the fact of his great esteem among the populace. All of these point to positive responses to their experience with him. For them, his presence in the desert was a sign that this man whose dress and comportment proved so strange and disturbing, was indeed clothed in the robes of the prophet. It was they who saw that his call to Israel was a sign that this desert had been conquered, for that was the other side of the equation: it was in the desert that Israel had come to know God!

Christian Origins, 13–20]), their strong group adhesion and alternate interpretation of Scripture provided the basis in "custom" needed for a secure existence.

These would have brought to mind a time in Israel's history when the desert experience was one of utmost grace. It was the time of the Exodus and Sinai, a short period to be sure, but the time of pilgrimage to the Holy Mountain where the people were to meet with their God to be given the grace of Torah. If immediately thereafter they were to fall into disfavor and bear the curse of wandering for forty years, their time at the foot of Sinai had made them God's people and served as a paradigm of the relationship with Yahweh which was to be effected in the land of promise, even as the forty years of trial stood as an actual mirror of what was in fact to transpire. That was the time when "Moses and Aaron, Nadab, and Abihu, and seventy of the elders of Israel went up, and . . . saw the God of Israel . . . and they beheld God, and ate and drank" (Exod 24:9-11 RSV). These were moments that were to be called to mind in sacred liturgy as foreshadowing a time of grace renewed. They were the moments of preparation, the other side of anomie and discontent—the side of the optimist, the side of one whose faith in God can lead to visions of the Spirit being poured out in the near future.

Repent and Be Baptized

Was John's presence in the desert to be seen in this light? Was it a call of judgment and grace at the same time; a call to Israel to now abandon the boundaries that had become indeed an obstacle to the kingdom for which she yearned? Was Israel once again to strip herself and go into the desert to meet once again the God who had called her so long ago?

Indeed the prophet Hosea had spoken of that day in which Yahweh would "allure her, and bring her into the wilderness, and speak tenderly to her" (RSV), and having cleansed her, once again make covenant. "And I will betroth you to me in righteousness and in justice," he said, "in steadfast love and in mercy. I will betroth you to me in faithfulness; and you shall know the Lord" (Hos 2:14, 19-20 RSV).

So too were the words of the prophet Jeremiah (2:2-3 RSV) clear and to the point:

Go and proclaim in the hearing of Jerusalem,
Thus says the Lord:

I remember the devotion of your youth
your love as a bride,
how you followed me in the wilderness,
in a land not sown.

Israel was holy to the Lord,
the first fruits of his harvest.
All who ate of it became guilty;
evil came upon them,
      says the Lord.

If our interpretation is correct, and all we have done is em-
phasized the other side of the coin that has always been interpreted in the light of Augustinian fatalism, then it was in this
tradition that John now stood in the desert as one victorious
and with the words of Isaiah on his lips:

A voice cries: . . .

"And the Glory of the Lord will be revealed
and all flesh shall see it together,
for the mouth of the Lord has spoken" (40:3, 5 RSV).

The evangelist Mark was later to picture Jesus in the same
spectrum, as he came out of the desert proclaiming the vic-
tory of God in the advent of his kingdom. John's was a call
to renewal; to drink once again the water of refreshment as
they had at Massah and Meribah, the place where for a proof
they knew that the Lord was among them (Exod 17:1-7).

"Behold, I am doing a new thing;
    now it springs forth, do you not perceive it?
I will make a way in the wilderness
    and rivers in the desert.
The wild beasts will honor me,
    the jackals and the ostriches;
for I give water in the wilderness,
    rivers in the desert,
to give drink to my chosen people,
    the people whom I formed for myself
that they might declare my praise" (Isa 43:19-21 RSV).

In a world where symbolic images and actions spoke so much more clearly than they do to us today, where prophetic tradition so often became the impetus for movements of renewal and reform, these associations were at hand and called for recognition. They were the heritage of Israel, the wellspring of culture that gave vitality to the life of even the most humble peasant, perhaps even more so than to the elite and the well read. It does our understanding of John no service to divorce him from his time because the literary texts do not seem to spell this out all so clearly. John was John, the first-century Jewish ascetic preacher, a peasant among peasants, whose movement produced no literature of its own, and who comes to us only in the shadow of his more famous disciple. The portrait we paint here reflects those origins far more accurately than any recourse to a comparative study of the literature of the elite of the time and our own ethnocentric criteria of authenticity could possibly afford. It gives us a new opening into understanding why Jesus, whose message can now be seen to be so much like that of John, was moved to accept his invitation to the desert to undergo his own "baptism of repentance."

John was clothed then, not in the garments of a madman or of the one who mourns for his own sins, but in those of the joyous desert prophet who announces to the nation the good news of salvation.[35] It is the triumphant voice of the Second Isaiah that stands as the horizon of interpretation for the work of John. He had gone out to the wilderness himself to "make straight the way of the Lord," that is, by his own witness, to seek and to find the God who was to be found there, for his dwelling place on the Holy Mount of Jerusalem seemed empty of his presence.[36] Why else would he have aban-

---

[35] As R. Pesch, *Das Markusevangelium* (Freiburg, Basel, Wien: Herder, I. 1976) 80–82, has pointed out, the description of the dress of John is not necessarily connected to any sort of Elijah model, but stems from the traditional garb of Bedouins and desert dwellers.

[36] Ezekiel 10 describes Yahweh's abandonment of the Temple, while Malachi 3:1b solemnly announces his return. Whether such a radical notion of God's absence (as is suggested in the Matthew 3:7-10 parallel) is to be attributed to John or any other of his contemporaries is a question that must be addressed below.

doned the priesthood? John's call from the desert was a power-
fully symbolic word to Israel to return with him to its roots
and thus stand purified for the visitation of its Lord.

For Isaiah this was an announcement of great joy, for it
marked the beginning of the return of Yahweh's people from
exile in Babylon. It was "in the desert" that the pathway was
to be made; a reliving of the Exodus, when God led his people
out of bondage to the Holy Mountain, there to make them a
people unto God. The vision was that having done that, now,
once again, they were to be led back, this time to a New Jerusalem,[37] there to manifest to all the world that Yahweh, their
God, was truly King. It was a powerful imagery, charged with
a fire that, given the circumstances, could not but cause a reaction. Indeed Good News for the poor!

But on the other hand, such a "gospel" could create difficulties for many and be no good news at all, since it suggested
that what Israel had heretofore engaged in was not "gospel"
at all. Thus the questions about who John was and where his
authority to preach these things came from became a burning
issue in the regions around the Jordan.

Since there is every reason to accept it as the earliest pattern
of interpretation applied to John, even as reflecting his own
self-understanding, we must wonder whether Matthew was
so far from correct when he summed up John's preaching with
"Repent, for the kingdom of heaven is at hand?"[38] It was—in
the desert, with him—to be met in the repentance baptism of
purifying fire that was administered in the saving waters of
the wilderness.[39] For all the redactional patterning that may

[37] Suggested Readings: Isaiah 40:1–55:13; 65:17-25; 66:1-24; Ezekiel
37:1-14 (40–48); Malachi 3:1-24; Zechariah 12:1–14:21; Revelation 21:1-27.

[38] This paralleling of the kingdom-preaching of John and Jesus is by
far and again considered a redactional peculiarity of Matthew by the
majority of exegetes. See, e.g., J. P. Maier, "John the Baptist in Matthew's
Gospel," *Journal of Biblical Literature* 99 (1980) 383–405.

[39] The probability is strong that the use of water-fire-Spirit image in reference to baptism was first applied to John (see Malachi 3:1-11; Zechariah
13:1-3; Ezekiel 36:25-26; 1Qs 4:20-21) and only separated into two dis-
tinct "kinds" of baptism within the Christian tradition. See R. Brown,
The Gospel According to John I, 51–54; J.D.G. Dunn, "Spirit-and-Fire Baptism," *Novum Testamentum* 14 (1972) 81–92.

be suggested here, there are no really convincing reasons to dismiss this possibility. In fact, it is in the context of the kingdom imagery and its relation with the desert tradition that the notion of repentance in these texts reaches its most profound level.

Summary

John's sudden appearance at the banks of the Jordan was perhaps one of the signs of the times that was assured to provide controversy for his own generation as well as for those that followed. Like the covenanters of Qumran, and indeed others throughout the history of the nation, he had taken up residence in a place fraught with meaning and ambiguity at the same time. But unlike them, he has left us no sign of the cause of his discontent. Even for his own contemporaries, his words were words which could divide as well as unite. How was one to read the signs that he performed? Was John's way of life and the preaching he did a sign that he was from God? Or was it rather evidence that he was a servant of the Evil One?

While he was not alone in calling for repentance and conversion, his uniqueness was to be found in his call to all of Israel to return to its roots in the wilderness. It was there that they were to discover, in the stark clarity of his summons, an invitation to create anew the Israel envisaged by the great prophet Isaiah some centuries before. Theirs was to be a time of trial and of grace, of justice-making and of love. For those who were to return to live in the hope of Isaiah, it was to be a time of gospel and the peace of God. Such a vision was not shared by everyone. And so they all came out, from the whole countryside and from Jerusalem. They came out to see and to hear, and perchance even to be washed in this water that he provided in the wilderness.

3

Servants of the Kingdom

Reading the Gospels can be a very challenging experience for people in our generation. There is so much going on in the narrative itself that one barely dares to probe below the surface of the text to seek the dialogue that gave it birth and sustained it to maturity. Yet that is where so many of its treasures lie!

There has been a great deal of discussion in recent years about what it means to say that a text is a form of communication.[1] As such, a text is said to imply and indeed to invite its readers to dialogue. Of course, sacred texts have always done that. It is the question of their appropriation and of their relevance to succeeding generations of believers. In their haste to enter into dialogue with the text of the New Testament, however, contemporary readers often fail to pause long enough to listen to what the text, for its part, has to say. It often comes as quite a surprise to find that the text speaks a language very different from their own. If contemporary readers have difficulty engaging the text, it is often because they must first struggle to understand that language, and come to grips with the way it reflects the culture of the people who used it to express and dialogue with their own experience and tradition. For if the text speaks to us at all, it speaks not only of, but from

[1] See chapter 1, n. 5.

the past, bringing us into a world not our own. If there is a dialogue to be had, therefore, it is one that has already begun, a dialogue that the contemporary reader enters from outside, and only at great risk. To become sensitized to the dialogue which produced the text and the tradition which sustains it in its ongoing life within a community, then, is to take the first necessary step in placing oneself within a legitimate context for interpretation and response.

This fact alone presents many believers with great difficulty, as they discover the tension between the traditions they have received and the challenges that this approach to the text presents. Of course, in the process, the Bible seems to have become so much more complex. For some, there is even the fear that it is being robbed of its life-giving vitality. There is a temptation to withdraw into a monologue, speaking about the text, but never coming to grips with the dynamic exchange that it reflects, or that it has provoked in the past life of the communities which hold it dear, and in turn can provoke in the contemporary reader. For the root question thrust upon us seems to be this: To what extent is that ancient text still able to answer the questions which we, in our generation, bring to it? Indeed, in a more specifically religious context, what does it mean for a modern reader to be a faithful hearer of the word?

In his work, *Against the Heresies*, the second-century bishop Irenaeus of Lyons stressed the fact that the Gospels of Matthew, Mark, Luke, and John were historically rooted in the tradition of the Apostles.[2] It was this rootedness in the past that made those Gospels, and none others, the starting point of any dialogue that was to be carried out in his own generation. Irenaeus was fighting a battle on two fronts. On the one hand there were the Marcionists, who had rejected all of the Church's Scriptures, except for their own expurgated versions of Paul and Luke; and on the other, there were the Gnostics, who had multiplied the sacred texts beyond any limits at all. Irenaeus' exercise in literary criticism sought to establish a communal context for understanding the Gospels as a buttress against a developing tide of antihistoricism, which threatened

[2] Book III. 1–5.

to sweep away the incarnational view of reality that Christianity had adopted.

His work also points to the fact that literary and historical criticism of the Gospels is almost as old as the works themselves. But the principles directing and informing their practice have changed throughout history. Often enough these were determined by the ideological necessities of the day, a fact which is often imperiously bemoaned by contemporary critics. But it is precisely this inherent characteristic which makes any research viable and worthy of engagement in the ongoing dialogue of town and gown. Within this context, however, the "scientific" study of the New Testament is a relatively modern phenomenon, developed in response to the challenges of the Enlightenment and Rationalism and based on the model of the so-called hard sciences.[3] The use of contemporary forms of historical criticism, despite its drawbacks and limitations, has opened a new window of opportunity for us to understand not only the text of the New Testament, but the life of the communities which stand behind those texts. We are thereby in the position to go beyond the dialogue between text and community which has been the meat of exegesis and theology for so long, and to come to a deeper appreciation of the dynamic interaction between the faith, life, and culture of those communities who gave us the Scriptures in the first place. It remains for us, of course, to grasp hold of these new insights and to integrate them into the work of appropriation.

The great exegete and theologian Origen, who was at the center of the exegetical debates at the beginning of the third century, urged his audiences that, if the Scriptures were to make any sense at all in their lives, they needed above all to be seriously studied. "Diligently apply yourself to the reading of the sacred scriptures," he wrote to the young Gregory,[4]

[3] See E. Guttgemanns, *Offene Fragen zur Formesgeschichte des Evangeliums. Eine methodische Skizze der Grundlagen der Form und Redaktionsgeschichte,* 2nd ed. (Munich: Kaiser, 1971).

[4] This letter was written to Gregory in about A.D. 230 before he was baptized. Later he was to become the bishop of neo-Caesarea and is known as Gregory the Wonder-Worker.

"I say apply yourself! For we who read the things of God need much application, lest we say or think anything too rashly about them. And applying yourself in this way to the study of the things of God . . . knock at its locked door, and it will be opened to you by the porter."[5] The modern reader should expect no less.

Baptized in Repentance

Perhaps some of the most fruitful texts for this kind of study are those that are concerned with John the Baptist. Each of the Synoptic Gospels begins its story of Jesus with the narrative of his baptism by John. "At that time," Mark tells his readers,

> "Jesus came from Nazareth in Galilee
> and was baptized by John in the Jordan.
> And when he came up out of the water,
> he saw the heavens split open
> and the Spirit descending like a dove on him.
> And a voice came from heaven,
> 'You are my beloved son;
> in you I am well pleased.' "

Quite an event, to be sure! For the early Christians, this was a divine affirmation of their belief in the status and mission of Jesus as Messiah and Son of God.

But the wonder of the description often turns our attention away from the stark facts of the case, facts that for years were to present a challenge to the Church. Jesus was baptized by John, the Son of God by the son of Zachary.

For the evangelist Mark, the relationship between John and Jesus is quite straightforward. John is the beginning of the Gospel, the one whose word, work, and destiny prepare the way for the One who was to come after him. There is a solidarity between them without which John's life has no meaning. But John is the lesser of the two, and the fact of his baptism of Jesus quickly fades into the shadows as the evangelist turns his attention to the astounding events which follow.

[5] Text from *Ante-Nicene Fathers*, IV, 393–394.

The heavens are split open to reveal the very Spirit of God descending gently[6] upon Jesus. A voice sounds from the open heavens, speaking intimately to him with the images of Scripture, images of royalty, humility, and sacrifice.[7] It is a wonderful story which announces the true identity of this Jesus as the Spirit-filled Servant and Son of God, who himself must struggle with the power of Satan before he enters upon his victorious proclamation of the gospel (Mark 1:12-14). The mystery that is thus revealed is not for Jesus, nor indeed for those on the banks of the Jordan, but for the readers of the Gospel, the Christian believers for whom Mark was writing, who had themselves to struggle with the meaning of his life and death. It is this revelation which is the center of the Gospel, a divine mystery which provides the reader with insight into every movement within the narrative which follows. At the same time, the readers of the Gospel are challenged to see that the mystery of their own Christian existence unfolds in that story. Theirs is life at the cutting edge of the kingdom, a life of proclamation whose meaning is hidden in the bitter suffering of rejection and violence.

For Mark, John's proclamation is of a "baptism of repentance for the forgiveness of sins" (Mark 1:4). In undergoing John's prophetic rite, Jesus, the beloved Son, is shown to be in solidarity not only with John, but with all those for whom he "came to give his life in ransom" (Mark 10:45). So Mark, in further referring to Jesus' death as a "baptism which I must undergo," promises both a share in that fate and the fruit of its endurance to those who would follow him (Mark 10:38-39). Such solidarity is the "stuff" of the Second Gospel and the powerful challenge that Mark provides to all who would read his book.

---

[6] If the phrase "as a dove" *(hos peristeran)* in Mark 1:10 is to be taken in an adverbial sense, then what is described would be the mode of the Spirit's descent and not its appearance, i.e., the Spirit descends "as a dove would." See L. Keck, "The Spirit and the Dove," *New Testament Studies* 17 (1970) 41–67; here, 63–67.

[7] Psalm 2:7, Isaiah 21:1 and Genesis 22:2 are the scriptural allusions which are brought together in v. 11.

In Matthew's Gospel, however, there are indications that a new problem had arisen within the community. Mark's Gospel had seemingly left too many questions unanswered so that the dialogue with the tradition which had begun when he first took pen to hand had now to enter into a new stage of development. For one, the question of the baptism of Jesus by John created a greater problem than it had for Mark. Indeed, the entire question of baptism itself seems to have become an issue in the Church of Matthew.[8] And so they are assured by the scriptural necessity of it all. "It is fitting for us to fulfill all righteousness" (RSV), Jesus answers, as much to them as to John, who, in his own reticence, has summarized the confusion of the later community. "I need to be baptized by you," he had protested, "but do you come to me?" (RSV). Now, if Jesus was baptized by John, how much more must his followers submit themselves to the rite which is enjoined upon them as the unifying sign of their faith and mission.[9] "Go and make disciples from every nation," he is said to have told them, "Baptize them in the name of the Father, and of the Son, and of the Holy Spirit" (Matt 28:19).[10] This is the baptism that John had promised, the Messiah's baptism in Holy Spirit and fire (Matt 3:11). It was now to be the Way which the Lord himself had provided for all into the righteousness of the kingdom.

In Luke, John seems barely even to enter the picture, for the great theophany occurs, Luke tells us, when Jesus was at prayer, after being baptized with all the people (Luke 3:21). The evangelist has already told us that John was in prison, and thus has been able to minimize the role that John played at Jesus' baptism.[11] Even earlier he was able to forestall the diffi-

---

[8] Wink, *John the Baptist*, 36–37.

[9] It is perhaps significant that Matthew makes no reference to repentance in connection with the rite. For his community of Jews and Gentiles, baptism had become the important ritual moment which clearly marked a person's change of status vis-à-vis the Church. The initiate thus crosses the boundary lines separating communities.

[10] This is clearly an ecclesiastical formulation whose Trinitarian as well as universalistic elements reflect a second-generation level of development within the Gentile Church.

[11] Josef Ernst, *Johannes der Täufer*, 100–101.

culty that Matthew faced by having Elizabeth proclaim to Mary, "But who am I that the mother of my Lord should come to me? The moment your greeting sounded in my ears, the baby leapt in my womb for joy" (Luke 1:43-44 NAB).

The Fourth Gospel's attempt to meet a similar difficulty within its own tradition is perhaps a bit rougher at the edges, for it simply omits any story of Jesus' baptism altogether, and presents John as the prophetic witness to the descent of the Spirit on the one who himself will "baptize with the Holy Spirit" (1:33 NAB).[12] "I confess I did not recognize him," says the Baptist, "though the very reason I came baptizing with water was that he might be revealed to Israel" (1:31 NAB).

While such statements often seem of little help in providing an explanation of the problem of the Messiah's undergoing a baptism at the hands of John, at least to the modern mind, perhaps it was all that was needed.

At any rate, there it is: indications in the text of a close dependence of Jesus upon John connected with John's rite of baptism. How telling it is, then, that while the evangelists to a man take pains to separate Jesus from John, at the same time they are not able to tear apart the memory of their time together. Each of the evangelists has presented this relationship in a new light, based on his overall presentation of the ministry of Jesus, some with more success than the others. But it is just this problematic nature of the tradition that has convinced even the most skeptical of modern scholars that the baptism of Jesus by John is indeed one of the most reliable historical traditions of the Gospels.[13]

We must beware, then, not to let the Christology of the baptism scenes, with their intricate use of the Hebrew Scriptures and their function in the various Gospels, conceal the importance of the fact that Jesus came out to the Jordan River to undergo baptism and become a part of the movement inaugurated by John. Within the early Church it was this histori-

---

[12] "(Jesus') baptism is for John's sake, so that John might recognize the Lamb of God." Wink, *John the Baptist*, 104.

[13] An exception to this is M. Enslin, "John and Jesus," *Zeitschrift für die neutestamentliche Wissenschaft* 66 (1975) 1–18. Enslin's arguments, however, are overstated and have not proven to be convincing.

cal relationship between John and Jesus that was to necessitate the struggle over the meaning of John in the plan of God and the role that he played vis-à-vis Jesus, their Lord and Messiah. But these were later difficulties that were bound to arise given the developments within the ministry of Jesus and his movement. Far from negative, this association was in fact bound to preserve the status of the Baptist and to bring him into a place of prominence in Christianity that he would not otherwise have had in the annals of history. At any rate, John's influence on Jesus and his followers cannot be lightly dismissed or downplayed in any way.

It is not by chance, then, that the tradition is so unanimous in beginning its story of Jesus with his baptism by John. That is the way it happened. While the texts themselves may still struggle with the relationship between the two, there can be no doubt that the baptism of Jesus at the hands of John is meant to stand at the head of the preaching of the life, death, and resurrection of the Messiah as the gospel of the Christian Church. What began in history thus becomes the theological starting point of the gospel as well. It is this interaction between history and theology, moreover, which stands at the basis of the Christian notion of incarnation, not only that of Jesus, but of the Church and her Scriptures as well. Irenaeus had understood this well!

He Is Elijah!

On one occasion, Jesus is said to have posed a question to the crowds that came to hear him: "What did you go out into the desert to see?" he asked (Matt 11:7; parallel Luke 7:24). It is a very likely question, one that almost had to be asked. As presented in Matthew's Gospel, it is part of a dynamic exchange that begins with a question posed by the disciples of John. "Are you 'the One who is to Come' or shall we look for another?" The ultimate climax of the dialogue is Jesus' invitation, "Come to me . . . take my yoke upon you . . . and you shall have rest for your souls" (Matt 11:28-29). It is important to note, therefore, that the material on the Baptist that is gathered together here in chapter 11 of Matthew's Gospel is used by the evangelist not merely to tell his readers about John, but to present a comparison between the person of John and that of Jesus and to invite them ultimately to a following of Jesus, who now, as teacher, offers them a place in the kingdom which John himself had earlier proclaimed (Matt 3:2).

The dynamic which stands behind the entire chapter on the redactional level seems to be that which, *mutatis mutandis,* is reflected in the narrative itself. John was now removed from the scene (he was in prison). In whom were those who had heard and responded to him now to find "rest for their souls?" Who indeed was this Jesus who now appeared in his place? What did he have to offer? While the immediate setting of John sending his disciples to question Jesus may be the work of an early redactor (to "Q"), the answer provided by the evangelist may surely be based on the words of Jesus and his disciples to the followers of John. But they go beyond the narrative to the readers of the book, inviting all those who were now, in a new generation, seeking a renewed Israel to find their rest in the teaching of Jesus. It is a perfect example of the way the Gospels are able to make their tradition speak in new times and circumstances.

Before we look more closely at the components of this text, however, we should take a look at another where a similar concern is voiced by Jesus, this time about himself. "Who do people say that I am?" he asks (Mark 8:27). "They replied, 'Some, John the Baptizer, others, Elijah, still others, one of the prophets.' " (NAB). In the Gospel of Mark, Jesus' question and the answers of the disciples become the dramatic centerpoint of the entire Gospel narrative, for Jesus pushes on in his questioning to elicit the faith-filled confession of Peter, "You are the Messiah!" There is recognition here that had not been elicited before, and the Gospel now builds on this statement of faith to complete its presentation of the true nature of that Messiahship and its relevance for the faith of the community.

The parallel text in Matthew (16:13-23) is expanded beyond that of Mark into a confession of the divine sonship of Jesus, a confession which is further characterized as a revelation from God and the foundation of the life of the Church. "You are the Christ, the Son of the Living God!" "Blessed are you, Simon, son of John," Jesus answers, "for flesh and blood has

not revealed this to you, but my Father who is in heaven!''
(RSV). It is in this confession of faith that Peter stands as the
image of the Church, the rock against which the powers of evil
shall not prevail.

Because of its position and importance in the structure of the
Gospels with their proclamation of Christian faith in the Messiah, Jesus' question and the responses of the disciples have
been generally studied at the level of the redaction of the evangelists. Little is granted to the historical substratum of this text,
if indeed it is considered at all. But a developing understanding of patterns of interaction among first-century populations
suggests that perhaps more credence ought to be given such
incidents as these. They are ''at home,'' so to speak, in the
milieu of the first-century peasant society of Jesus.

Whereas we in our generation are often urged not to pay
attention to what people may say, in the first century, it was
critical to do just that. One's personal identity, or perhaps to
put it better, one's self-worth was tied up precisely with
people's perceptions, for a person was always considered in
relation to others in his or her life, their identity found in their
embeddedness in the group to which they belonged.[14] Stereotyped role-playing was therefore a very important personal and
social program and could have serious consequences for acceptance and recognition within society. It was not a sham,
but rather called for an interiorization of roles which would
shape a person's life in community. Thus the perception of
others could play a large role in a person's relationship with
the rest of society and the effectiveness of their words.

Despite our own emphasis on individuality and individualism, we often experience something of the same thing in our
own day. For us, however, this ''game that people play'' is
looked upon with a certain distaste because it is often used
in our culture for personal precedence and power-grabbing.
Perhaps it is this that makes us uncomfortable at discovering
that it may have played such a prominent role in the life of
Jesus. In his society its purpose was far different from what

---

[14] For a discussion of the notion of dyadic person see B. Malina, *The
New Testament World: Insights from Cultural Anthropology* (Atlanta: John
Knox, 1981) 51–70.

it has assumed in our own. At any rate, the importance of this interest in other people's reaction is certainly borne out by the vast number of Christological titles that the New Testament uses. What we are suggesting is that the same interest that we find in the early Church concerning the identity of Jesus was already evident during his lifetime. Its roots lie not simply in the soil of Christian theological speculation or creedal proclamation, but in that of cultural patterning. That others should be concerned with the true identity of Jesus and the meaning of his activities vis-à-vis his own contemporaries, so much so that they would use images and comparisons to label him, and that he himself would in turn respond to that process, is a typical first-century pattern of challenge-response, (used, in this case, to "get a fix" on him), that must be taken seriously as the basis for any discussion of texts such as these.[15]

Why bring all that up here? Partly because the same dynamic applies to John and his relationship to his contemporaries. In the case of John, however, we have to dig a little deeper to hear what is going on. "Some say that you are Elijah, or John the Baptist, or one of the prophets," Jesus' disciples answer him. Was this a real event? Did it ever really happen, or was it composed in the workshop of the evangelist, as is so often claimed? It would seem that there is every reason to suspect that the narrative does indeed reflect the peasant reactions to Jesus' ministry, perhaps even their recognition of some sort of "messianic status" for him. After all, there was no single idea of who the Messiah was to be, and unlikely as it was that he would fit the bill for the more traditional conceptions of messianism, there were other possibilities ready at hand.[16]

But our concern here is directed more to the first part of the disciples' answer. Notice that Jesus is likened in the popular

---

[15] See Bruce J. Malina and Jerome H. Neyrey, *Calling Jesus Names: The Social Value of Labels in Matthew* (Sonoma, California: Polebridge, 1988).

[16] Two studies of the various currents of messianic thought in the Judaism of this time are those of Richard A. Horsley and John P. Hanson, *Bandits, Prophets, and Messiahs* (New York: Winston/Seabury, 1985), and Jacob Neusner, William Scott Green and Ernest S. Frerichs, eds., *Judaisms and Their Messiahs at the Turn of the Christian Era* (New York: Cambridge University, 1987).

mind to Elijah, to John the Baptist, to the prophets! For the New Testament none of those designations is sufficient, but their inclusion here indicates that all of them were indeed possible answers to the question. In fact, each gives witness to a positive recognition of Jesus as one possessed of God's spirit, a prophet like Elijah or John or one of the other spirit-filled persons of their tradition (note how the tradition of Matthew feels free to add even Jeremiah to the list). They stand in sharp contrast to the charges made against him in another place by those who saw his ministry in more negative terms, "he is possessed by Beelzebub and it is by the prince of demons that he does these things" (Mark 3:22).

What is important for our investigation at this point is that Jesus could be compared to John the Baptist and placed within the company of Elijah and the Prophets. Does this mean that John, in his turn, was considered as being among the Prophets, perhaps an Elijah of sorts? One would be hard-pressed to deny it. As we have seen, there are other indications as well that indeed that was the case.

"What did you go out into the desert to see?" As is so often the case in the Gospels, Jesus answers for them. Surely they would all agree with him that it was not simply to see "a reed shaken by the wind." They were not on a scenic tour! Nor did they go out to see "a man clothed in the robes of royalty." Indeed, either of these would have been quite attractive to the peasants of Judea, who would have possessed barely two sticks to rub against each other. They would have provided a welcome diversion to the rather humdrum regularity of their lives. Or perhaps the reference is even more pointed, directing the audience to individuals who might tease them for their allegiance; movers and shakers within Israel, those who in the eyes of Jesus (and of John) had perverted the true nature of God's kingdom. But no, it was not these who had drawn the people, for such were not to be found in the wilderness places. They had gone out to see someone whom they considered a prophet, someone who had spoken the text of the desert. That was the attraction of John and at the same time the challenge that those who now surrounded Jesus had accepted. For them, he was indeed "a man sent by God" (John 1:6).

Yet Jesus seems to go even beyond this in his praise of John. For Jesus, John was even more than a prophet. Surely, he was authorized by God (Mark 11:27-33; Matt 21:23-27), but "of those born of woman," he was to say, "there has risen no one greater." We must be careful not to read too much of a theological nature into this answer. There is little radical eschatology here! It represents the kind of exaggerated comparisons that are common in Mediterranean culture, and it serves here as a foil to the the final part of Jesus' answer which fulfills the evangelist's ultimate purpose of Christian proclamation. "Even the least in the kingdom is greater than John!"[17]

Nevertheless, the statement itself surely reflects something of Jesus' own reaction to John. Why else would he have submitted to his baptism, had he not understood it as representing the will of God? It is, however, a provocative statement, especially if John had been as controversial as he is pictured to have been. It is a statement which takes sides in a controversy. It is meant to raise questions—to set a challenge before the audience and to play a role in the ongoing discourse about the honor of John and to set him into a new context with his own (Jesus') ministry. As we have seen, it was not only the later Christians who would have been concerned with such questions!

What does it mean then to say that John was such a great prophet? See how urgent the statement is: There has never arisen anyone who was greater than the one whom you have followed! It reflects the urgency of those involved in a present reality. These were the people who had responded to the prophet. Of course he was the greatest, for his words had been for them. Now was the time of God's visitation. What remained was only for it to be manifest to all! On the lips of Jesus these words about John become even more important to the crowds who were attracted to him than any other consideration. By heaping such praise upon John, Jesus avoids the kind of challenge-encounter about the Baptist that his own preaching could provoke. He thus maintains the honor which John

[17] Wink (*John the Baptist*, 25) understands this as a community construction.

had won among the people, while at the same time being able legitimately to replace him in the loyalty of his followers.[18]

The final answer that Matthew provides in this quest for the meaning of John is probably one that took time to be formulated such as it is, for it is marked by the clear Christological concerns of the early Church. Nevertheless, that does not preclude a rooting of its imagery in the ministry of Jesus.

"He is the one of whom it is written," says Jesus,

> "Behold I send my messenger before thy face
> who shall prepare thy way before thee' " (RSV).[19]

The original form of the quotation is said to be taken from the Book of Malachi, the last in the Old Testament canon of the prophets. Malachi indeed is presented as the messenger of Yahweh (mal'aki = my messenger), the model of the true priest (2:7), who as prophet would prepare Israel for the return of her God, who alone could purify the priesthood so that a true and pleasing sacrifice could once again be offered.[20] In fact, the prophecies of Malachi were to call for the constant renewal of the nation and the institutions which served it. This was the work of prophecy. There is nothing particularly "eschatological" about it, at least not in the "end-of-the-world" sense

[18] For another approach to this discourse see R. Cameron, "What Have You Come Out To See? Characterizations of John and Jesus in the Gospels," *Semeia* 49 (1990) 35–69, who applies a rhetorical model derived from Greco-Roman school practice to the text. For Cameron this discourse represents an elaboration of a Chreia "which sought to ally Jesus and John as envoys of Wisdom, founders said to be vindicated along with their followers despite being rejected by their contemporaries." Cameron's confident assertions about the fit of the model are not always as obvious or convincing as he portrays them. Nevertheless, the theme of legitimacy (honor) looms large in his analysis also.

[19] Malachi 3:1 reads "Behold I send my messenger to prepare the way before me, and the Lord whom you seek will suddenly come to his temple; the messenger of the covenant in whom you delight, behold, he is coming, says the Lord of hosts" (RSV).

[20] Norman K. Gottwald, *The Hebrew Bible: A Socio-Literary Introduction* (Philadelphia: Fortress, 1985) 468–469. The possibilities of interpretation of this verse are discussed by B. V. Malchow, "The Messenger of the Covenant in Mal 3:1," *Journal of Biblical Literature* 103 (1984) 252–255.

that that word has acquired in much of recent theology.[21] The imminence of God was a constant concern of his people. Each of his expected visitations, in its time, was seen as final, only to be pushed back into the collective memory as life, as it were, went on. For the "presence of God" never seemed to be a manifest reality in the life of the nation; "prophetic dissonance" it has been called. But in Malachi 4:5 (3:23) the image is made more concrete by a later redactor who, in an attempt to save the prophecy for a new generation, had referred to the prophet Elijah, taken up to heaven in a whirlwind (2 Kings 2:1-12). It was this prophet who, as it were, still had one foot on the ground, for he had not yet passed through death. Standing as the final figure in the collection of prophetic oracles, he leaves open the hope of yet another revelation of Yahweh to his people, surely the final and great Day of the Lord, which would bring his plan to completion.[22] His task was to be the restoration of justice and peace to a nation where they could no longer be found, "to turn the hearts of the fathers to their children, and the hearts of the children to their fathers" (RSV).

If then, the crowds were attracted to John, it was because they were able to find reflected in him and in his teaching the principal aspirations that they themselves shared as children of the covenant. He was, in the radical sense of the term, "one of them." He was greater than a prophet and, according to Matthew, greater even than Elijah, because he embodied those ideals over which that prophet stood guard. He called from the past, but was as present to them as they were to themselves. His very being inspired confidence in his hearers because he was able to articulate in his word and work the very depths of their longing. To accept John as Elijah was to recognize him as the representative and protector of their cultural values and aspirations.

Theirs was an expectation of finality which must be seen within the context of a society marked by an abiding aware-

[21] Marcus J. Borg, *Conflict, Holiness & Politics in the Teachings of Jesus* (New York and Toronto: Edwin Mellen, 1984) especially chapter 1.
[22] It is perhaps this very factor which had placed the Book of Malachi as the last of the books in the canon of prophetic Scriptures.

ness of the present.[23] The children of Israel did not look to-ward the future, but toward their own immediate experience. If the prophet was calling in the wilderness and offering bap-tism, it signaled a new experience of Yahweh's activity on their behalf. They need not look to the imaginary future. That was known only to God. The voice of the Prophet signaled the present reality, to be grasped in the present through the sym-bolic recognition of him as a man sent by God. To recognize him as prophet was to ascribe to him the authority to call the community to conversion. It justified their own sense that such was indeed necessary. Such a sense of authority emerged from the prophet's ability to move his hearers to recognize his own position as superior to that of the officially legitimate authorities in the land. And it is this recognition which is sanctioned by the allusion to the great prophet Elijah and the Holy Scriptures.

"Some people say that you are Elijah," Peter had responded to Jesus. When now the disciples of John came to ask Jesus if he was "The One Who is to Come," Jesus does not answer directly, but points obliquely to the same complex of Isaianic prophecies[24] that John himself had used and that would be used as a paradigm of interpretation in the early Church. "Go back and report to John what you have seen and heard. The blind recover their sight, cripples walk, lepers are cured, the deaf hear, dead men are raised to life, and the poor have the good news preached to them" (NAB). These are the Scriptures which set the parameters for interpreting the activity of Jesus. What may seem at first to be a paradigm shift in fact builds on the model already provided. For it is in the description of "what (they) hear and see" that the justice and peace which Malachi had called for are now manifest.

"Blessed is the one," Jesus continues as they take their leave of him, "who takes no offense at me." Within its immediate context, the text can refer to none other than John, who had sought a clarification about Jesus in the first place. For the reader of the Gospel, however, the affair is only settled when

[23] See Bruce J. Malina, "Christ and Time: Swiss or Mediterranean?" *Catholic Biblical Quarterly* 51 (1989) 1–31.

[24] (Isaiah 29:18-19; 35:5-6; 61:1).

Matthew has Jesus, who had pointed to John as the "Elijah who is to come," quote from the collection of Christian testimonies on his behalf. For the Elijah of whom Jesus spoke had indeed come before their Lord and Master. The prophetic hope enshrined in the final words of the canon of the Prophets was now fulfilled. What a marvelous exchange the evangelist has narrated. The holy Prophets of Israel give voice to their presence among yet a new generation. "Prepare the way of the Lord. Make his paths straight!"

The Baptizer and the Baptized

"What did you go out into the desert to see?" If Jesus was able to ask that of the people who had come out to hear his teaching, it was only because he himself had gone out to see and to hear, and even to accept baptism at the hands of John. At the end of his "infancy account," where the relationship between Jesus and John is so dramatically portrayed, Luke tells us that Jesus "grew in wisdom and age and grace before God and man" (Luke 2:52). He does not tell us, however, how much of that wisdom and grace was to come from John. None of the Gospels directly tells us that. But it is not an idle question to ask.

It is a question, however, that many Christians refuse to entertain. It is almost as though it were unworthy of their belief in the Son of God. Yet orthodox Christianity has always struggled with the question of limitation and growth in the life of Jesus and has cherished that struggle as a sign of faithfulness to its understanding of his humanity. What we are looking to understand in such questioning is not what separates Jesus from John, but what unites them. A pressing question—in fact, a vital one for the Churches, perhaps more vital than any on the other side of the equation, for an emphasis on the formulae of faith has often left modern Christians in the position of the Docetists, who, in their own time had failed to come to grips with the humanity of their Savior and were thus unprepared for the incredible onslaught of Gnostic fantasy that overwhelmed so many in the later part of the second century.

At the same time, such work is often fraught with the dangers of romanticism heightened by a reticence toward the incarnational character of the Sacred Scriptures which has led to a fundamentalist security in faith that can be nothing if not destructive of the humanity of its adherents.

But perhaps it is also true that these are questions that cannot be completely answered. Even the great Saint Augustine had to face that possibility time and again in his preaching about the Scriptures. But even he had to admit, "If these things were not cloaked in mystery, they would never be carefully scrutinized." The very opaqueness of the text insistently demanded that the reader make every effort at finding solutions to the problems it presented. These were the "closed pages of the Sacred Scriptures" to which Origen had alluded. For Augustine, they were to be read (even) in public specifically "so that the soul would be spurred on to study them." For it was only with such study, he was convinced, that the discovery of what they actually contained could "yield such delight."[25] The intellectual challenges of faith were Augustine's very lifeblood. Yet for Augustine it was the eternal mystery of God that the text revealed, a mystery without which no one could be in possession of the truth which he so desperately sought.

The Synoptic Gospels present Jesus as beginning his ministry in Galilee only after the arrest of the Baptist. Nothing more is directly said of the relationship between the two during their ministry, nor of that of their disciples. Nevertheless, modern scholarship has often proposed that much of the gospel tradition concerning John was developed against the background of a kind of rivalry between the two groups, if not during the lifetime of Jesus, then certainly afterwards, when their respective leaders were each proclaimed as Messiah. In fact Jesus himself is often seen as having separated from John precisely because of a difference in understanding of the "time of the kingdom." Was there such a rivalry between them as we so often are led to believe? Or were their ministries, in fact, inextricably joined together, only to be severed by the passing of time and the force of destiny?

[25] Sermon 60/A, 1, cf. John Rotelle, ed., *The Works of Saint Augustine, A Translation for the 21st Century. Sermons, I* (Brooklyn: New City Press, 1990) 36.

According to the tradition, it would seem that upon enter-ing Galilee, Jesus was soon joined in his ministry by as un-likely a group of peasants as could ever come together. There was Peter, the impulsive fisherman, who was to serve a num-ber of times as a kind of spokesman for the group (Mark 8:29), and his brother Andrew; James and his brother John, whose ambition within the group was to cause no little resentment (Mark 10:35-41); Matthew, the tax collector (Mark 2:14); Judas, and a host of others about whom we know nothing except that they were there. None seems to have been particularly noteworthy—actually, the tradition seems to stress that very fact.

Their following was, in many ways, filled with ambiguity and rivalry, and finally ends in an ultimate betrayal and aban-donment. One can hardly speak about the undying loyalty of the disciples of Jesus! Certainly there was nothing to recom-mend them as followers of so great a master! What could it have been that would have attracted the kind of following that he seems to have had? What was going on?

The Synoptic tradition stresses that Jesus had, in fact, chosen his own disciples. According to Mark, Jesus chose them, "to be with him and to share in his ministry" (3:14-15); he gave them special instruction and insight into his teaching (Mark 4:10), and to some, even a share in those intimate mystical experiences which are at the base of some of the most mys-terious stories in the Gospels (Mark 9:2-9; 14:39-49). At one moment Peter is able to make a confession of confidence, "You are the Messiah" (Mark 8:29); yet, not very long afterwards, he was to "swear with the strongest oaths, 'I do not know this man that you are talking about' " (Mark 14:71). Had he chosen the wrong lot? "Do you not yet see nor understand?," Jesus was to ask them. "Are your minds so dull? When you have eyes can you not see, and when you have ears can you not hear?" (Mark 8:17-18). Jesus was alluding to Isaiah the prophet, who, after a long and seemingly fruitless career, was to look back and wonder if indeed his work had been all in vain (Isa 6:9-13). A moment of frustration, this, suffered by all who have a vision that challenges the status of things. Yet to his credit, Peter was to collapse in tears after the incident in the court-yard (Mark 14:72). One can only wonder at the poignancy of these scenes, painted so dispassionately in the Gospels, as if waiting to be captured on the canvasses of a later generation.[26] The stories are wonderful! Their impact has been profound!

In chapter 5 of Mark's Gospel there is a story about a different kind of disciple. It is the story of the man who was possessed by a whole legion of demons (Mark 5:1-20). He lives a miserable life, screaming and shouting among the tombstones, an obvious outcast from society. Whatever the illness the man suffered, its social consequences were devastating. The narrative is fascinating—one of the best in the Gospel for its color and movement! But perhaps the most important aspects of the story are often missed by its readers. After the man is healed, he asks Jesus if he could go with him; he wants to become a disciple. What better candidate? In these circumstances Jesus' response seems rather strange: "But (Jesus) would not permit it, but said to him, 'Go home to your own people, and tell them all the Lord has done for you and how he took pity on you' " (Mark 5:19). You see, the man was not a Jew. He was from the country of the Gerasenes, on the other side of the sea! Such an association as he sought would have been unthinkable in social terms. No, he cannot come after Jesus and follow him; nevertheless, he must (and does) go to his own people and tell them about the pity that the Lord, the God of Israel, has bestowed on him through the man Jesus. There is an interesting interplay here between the cultural reality of ethnic exclusivity that would have prevailed in the Palestine of Jesus' day and the universalism that so marked the latter stages of the Jesus movement in the period of the early Church. But that is another issue.

We single out this incident because it points to one of the many tensions we have to face in trying to reconstruct some kind of coherent picture of the early Jesus group. The traditions about "following Jesus" and "discipleship" are complex and have been studied extensively. Who are to be designated as disciples and followers of Jesus? Why did they follow him? Was it because he was an exorcist? The Gospels are filled with stories of his power over demons. But Matthew 12:27 suggests

[26] One thinks immediately of the wonderful painting *The Tears of Peter* by El Greco (1541–1614).

that he would not have been the only one to have had such powers![27] Or was he a miracle worker like the fabled Apolonius of Tyana, whose life, written by Philostratus, was to become a sort of rival to the Gospels? Or was it his powerful teaching that attracted them, much as that of the famous rabbi, Johannan ben Zakkai? Perhaps he was a bit of them all rolled into one?

In fact, the Gospels present Jesus as wearing all these hats during his brief public life, so that it becomes very difficult to discern which one fit him best. But the question we wish to pose has to do more with the disciples than with Jesus. If indeed, "they did not understand," why did they stay with him for so long? Certainly for Mark being a disciple meant being with Jesus. It was not imitation of the master but a literal "following after" him. In its turn, this story suggests that there was some sort of selectivity in the process of group formation![28] It was not for everyone, even in cases where one could expect a loyalty that would be nothing if not genuine. Was it merely ethnic solidarity or were there other factors at play? It becomes obvious that "Many are called, but few are chosen!" But who were these many? Who the few? And of course, what has all this to do with John the Baptist?

Once we begin to speak of the dynamics of a group, however, we enter once again into the world of the social sciences. Indeed, biblical studies has recently done just that, and with a vengeance. Actually there have been any number of attempts to understand this Jesus group as a social phenomenon and to characterize it according to one sociological pattern or another. And the results have often been applied to John and his group as well. One thinks immediately of Max Weber and his application of the charismatic model to Jesus.[29] But we must tread lightly here, for, as we have stressed, in the New Testament we are dealing with texts that come from a differ-

---

[27] "If I cast out demons by Beelzebul, by whom do your sons cast them out?" (RSV).

[28] Ethnic distinctions? Or does this stem from the evangelist's concern with looking back to the origins of the Gentile preaching?

[29] Max Weber, *Economy and Society*, trans. G. Roth and C. Wittich (Berkley: University of California, 1968 [1922]).

ent time and a different place than our own. Many contemporary "social science" approaches to the New Testament do not seem to take that distancing seriously enough. It does not seem helpful, for example, to discuss first-century Palestinian Jewish realities as if they were expressions of nineteenth- and twentieth-century European and North American experiences. We must question, then, how helpful it is to talk about John and Jesus as charismatic leaders, and their followers as charismatic groups,[30] or to speak of them in terms of sectarian division.[31] The parameters of social intercourse which inform those models simply are not evident in the texts we have, and in fact do not appear even today in the peasant societies of the Mediterranean basin. We will be better served to use models which arise from experiences which are closer to those realities themselves.[32]

While we have no sources which speak of the gathering of the disciples of John, each of the four Gospels almost goes out of its way to describe the gathering of the disciples of Jesus. As we have already intimated, the Synoptic Gospels make no connection at all between the disciples of John and those of Jesus. Instead, each narrates a story which sets them apart quite dramatically. Matthew follows Mark's account of the call of the disciples almost perfectly (Matt 4:18-22), while Luke artistically combines it with the tradition of the miraculous catch of fish which we find as a post-Easter appearance story in John's Gospel (Luke 5:1-11; John 21:1-11). All three, however, stress the presence of Peter, James, and John, who were to assume places of authority in the Jerusalem community after the death and resurrection of Jesus (Gal 2:9) and whose status was fixed

---

[30] John Gager, *Kingdom and Community: The Social World of Early Christianity* (Englewood Cliffs: Prentice Hall, 1975); Robin Scroggs, "The Earliest Christian Communities as Sectarian Movements," in Jacob Neusner, ed., *Christianity, Judaism and Other Greco-Roman Cults, (FS Morton Smith) II,* (Leiden: Brill, 1975) 1-23.

[31] For a summary and critique of the use of this category in recent New Testament literature see: Bengst Holmberg, *Sociology and the New Testament: An Appraisal* (Philadelphia: Fortress, 1989) 88-117.

[32] See here B. J. Malina, "Jesus as Charismatic Leader?" *Biblical Theology Bulletin* 14 (1984) 55-62.

by their presence in the tradition at significant moments in his life.[33]

The texts themselves call to mind many of the vocation narratives of the Old Testament,[34] but seem particularly to be modeled on the story of the call of Elisha by Elijah in 1 Kings 19:19-21. That is to say, they are presented as idealized narratives which stress the character of the call and the response that it elicits, and are meant to serve, perhaps primarily, as models for the kind of following the Christian reader is to undertake. It all seems rather mysterious. It is Jesus who initiates the relationship by himself calling the disciples. There is virtually no psychological interest at all in those who are called, their motivation, or the process of decision-making. The call is sudden and unexpected, the answer unquestioning, complete, decisive. It seems quite clear, then, that the picture that we have thus drawn in the Synoptics is already formed by an image of the later Church and its awareness of mission.

In the Gospel of John, however, a different picture emerges. Here the "Jesus Group" has its beginnings not in Galilee, but at the shores of the Jordan among the followers of the Baptist! It is in fact the Baptist who points out Jesus to two of his own disciples. "Look!" he says, "There is the Lamb of God" (NAB) thus beginning what turns out to be an ambiguous relationship between John, Jesus, and a group of people who formed a rather broad faction within the Judaism of the time. It is this ambiguity which clearly comes through in all of the texts and reflects the kind of binding, or lack of it, that would actually mark a political faction within the parameters of first-century Jewish society.[35] Of course Andrew's exclamation, "We have found the Messiah!" (NAB), sets the tone of the narrative within its Christian context, but the loose coherence of the group as a baptist movement, even after this proclamation, is

---

[33] Note first of all that the pericope is composed of two stories which have been simply but effectively put together: the one about Peter and Andrew, the other about James and John. This combination had perhaps been suggested by the prominence of Peter, James, and John in the tradition (see Mark 9:1-10; 14:32-42; Gal 2:9).

[34] Exodus 3:1-22; 1 Samuel 3:1-4:1; Isaiah 6:1-13; Jeremiah 4:4-19.

[35] Malina, "Jesus as Charismatic?"

an important social reality which is evidenced in the traditions that the evangelist uses. "Later on, Jesus and his disciples came into Judean territory, and he spent some time with them there baptizing" (John 3:22 NAB). John uses this tradition to expound on the subordination of the Baptist to Jesus, but here again the tradition itself cannot be explained away as a later redactor attempts in 4:2![36] It is simply not acceptable to dismiss the historical rootedness of these traditions in the ministry of John and Jesus or to impose later patterns of interpretation on them.

What was it that separated Jesus from John? It is our contention that the answer to this question is: Nothing! Rather, it would seem to be more of the very nature of the movement itself—popular, unstructured, reaching out to all who would hear—not to form a countergroup, but to adopt a new vision which would sweep up all in its wake. "All the Judean countryside and the people of Jerusalem went out to him in great numbers" (Mark 1:5 NAB), just as they were to do in the case of Jesus, and again, as the Book of Acts tells us, in the case of the first Christian preachers on the day of Pentecost (Acts 2:5-12). Their challenge was to all the people, to be extended as circumstances changed, so that in the consummation, it was to reach "the very ends of the earth" (Acts 1:8).

It is quite to the point, then, that it was only "after John was arrested, (that) Jesus came into Galilee proclaiming the Gospel of God" (Mark 1:14). Yes, the texts are marked by the "theology of the Evangelist." But they are just as surely marked by the "remembrance of the way it really was!"[37] What John

---

[36] As for Jesus' own baptismal activity, after having three times referred to it in the first days of his ministry, a later hand has simply inserted a corrective note at the beginning of chapter 4: "Now when the Lord knew that the Pharisees had heard that Jesus was making and baptizing more disciples than John *(although Jesus himself did not baptize, but only his disciples)*, he left Judea and departed again to Galilee."

[37] For a study of the chronological questions which would suggest a more rigid formulation of this relationship than that offered here see: W. Schenk, "Gefangenschaft und Tod des Täufers. Erwägungen zur Chronologie und ihren Konzequenzen," *New Testament Studies* 29 (1983) 453–483.

had begun in the regions of the desert of Judea was, after his death, to be taken by Jesus into the villages of Galilee. It is in this village manifestation that it flowers and finally moves, after Jesus' resurrection, into the cities of the Empire. Remembrance of the early pattern of the Baptist movement as a political faction, however, was in time to become obscured when it was removed from its cultural context in the sociopolitical realities of Palestinian Jewish life. John was soon to be seen, not as "the one of whom no greater has been born of woman," but as the one "unworthy to stoop down and untie the straps of his sandals." The roots of that change, however, are to be found not in the ministry of John, nor of Jesus, but in that of the early Christians whose communities were to develop according to the patterns of domestic religion and thus take on the contours of a pseudo-kinship system.[38]

Summary

The texts that we have examined up to now reflect an interest in the person of John and his role in the plan of God that was at the heart of Israelite piety, no matter what its formal realization may have been. Rather than presenting John as someone outside the borders of its experience, he is presented as being in continuity with the great figures of Israel's past. His call does not result in the formation of a group removed from society, but in a following which sees in him the impetus for a new vision of reality which in turn serves as the seedbed for the newness of the kingdom proclamation of Jesus and the early Church.

---

[38] See Bruce J. Malina, "Religion in the World of Paul," *Biblical Theology Bulletin* 16 (1986) 92–101.

4

Visions of the Kingdom

The Gospel in Galilee

It is one thing to see visions and to dream dreams, but quite another to have those visions and dreams accepted as the utterance of prophecy. If it is true that we use language to interpret our experience of the world, then the language of vision and dream often reflects worlds that are beyond the ability of observers to truly understand. How is one to respond to words that present a reality not our own? Should we rejoice and be glad, or should we rather rend our garments at the world created by such language? These are serious questions, which often can find no sure answer.

On the day of Pentecost, for example, when they heard the followers of Jesus praising God in a multitude of languages (Acts 2:13), the people of Jerusalem were told that the prophet Joel had foretold those events:

> "Your sons and daughters shall prophesy,
> your young men shall see visions,
> and your old men shall dream dreams" (Joel 3:1-5; Acts 2:17 RSV).

Yet for some, this "speaking in tongues" had nothing to do with the Spirit of God. "They are filled with new wine," was their response. If there was any spirit involved, it was the spirit of the vine!

What a blasphemy!

Or is it in the nature of things that those who dream dreams and see visions of "heavenly wonders" and "signs on the earth" are forever to be labeled "dreamers," and dismissed as being "beside themselves," possessed by Beelzebub, the "Prince of Demons" (Mark 3:22)?

John the Baptist was a dreamer, and for some of his contemporaries, a revealer of God's word. His vision was taken up by Jesus who was to tell his own disciples, "I saw Satan falling, like lightning, from heaven" (Luke 10:18 RSV).[1] This is surely a symbolic way of summing up the purport of that vision, charged with an imagery that grasped the reality of his own experience better than any other. The question was, however, whether anyone else could share in that vision and live its reality. For those who did, the dream that he offered to the outcasts and celebrated at his table was from God. His attempts to mold that dream into a new communal reality were the core of his proclamation of the kingdom. It was a dream based on the traditions which, on the one hand, were shared by the nation at large, but on the other, tore at the very heart of the reality that many of his contemporaries experienced. It was these latter ones who, no matter how much they looked and listened, were never really able to see and understand; for as Mark, in a fit of prophetic sarcasm, would have it, "they might perhaps repent, and be forgiven!" (Mark 4:12).

According to our earliest gospel, it was only after the death of John that "Jesus came into Galilee, proclaiming the Gospel of God" (Mark 1:14). Many years before Mark was to write those words, St. Paul had used the same sort of language in addressing his own communities.[2] It was this gospel, he writes,

---

[1] In its present context in Luke, the saying refers to the mission of the seventy-two disciples. According to J. Fitzmyer (*Luke* II, 850, with reference to J. Jeremias, *Die Sprache des Lukasevangeliums* [Göttingen: Vandenhoeck & Ruprecht, 1980] 187–189), "the strangeness of the saying may be the best reason for ascribing it to Jesus himself." Fitzmyer's discussion of the text is a most satisfying one.

[2] For an overview of Paul's use see G. Friedrich, in *Theological Dictionary of the New Testament* 2:729-734; P. Stuhlmacher, *Das paulinische Evangelium. I Vorgeschichte* (Göttingen: Vandenhoeck & Ruprecht, 1968).

that he had been "set aside" to proclaim (Rom 1:1; Gal 1:15-16), and had shared with them even in great affliction (1 Thess 1:6). For Paul, this gospel was indeed a revelation (Gal 2:16; 1 Thess 2:13). It was about God's Son, about his death for sin, and his being raised to glory (1 Cor 15:3-4). It was a revelation of God to be handed on "so that the Gentiles may be offered up as a pleasing sacrifice, consecrated by the Holy Spirit" (Rom 15:16 NAB).

While there is always a bit of ambiguity in the use of such language, perhaps that is the way it is intended. For to speak of the "gospel of God" can mean that the gospel which is being proclaimed comes from God, and therefore has the divine authority behind it; or it can mean that the gospel is about God, that is, about who God is and how God has acted in the history of God's people.[3] Much of the discussion of these texts over the years has presumed that the gospel writers were as precise in their distinctions as we often like to think we are, and so has struggled with deciding for one interpretation or the other.[4] But such precision is not always the case even in our own world of many cultures. One cannot help but suggest that the ambiguity which is inherent in the use of such grammatical constructions caused no difficulty to the ancient world, for it was able to perceive both meanings with neither coming off the worse for it![5] In any event, for our purposes, the situation would remain the same, for the language spoken claims to describe a divine reality, a reality beyond the realm of human experience.

If the Gospels use this word as a language of revelation, then the last phrase of their summary of Jesus' proclamation is as much a simple statement of fact as a call to reponse. "Repent and believe the gospel." Even in Mark, the repentance that John called for is taken up into the proclamation of the Church. What is called for on the part of the one who receives the words

[3] The difference would be between a subjective or an objective use of the genitive case in Greek.

[4] See, e.g., G. Dautzenberg, "Die Zeit des Evangeliums," *Biblische Zeitschrift* 21 (1977) 219–225.

[5] M. Zerwick, *Biblical Greek* (Rome: PIB, 1963) 36, speaks of a "general" use of the genitive case here.

about God is *metanoia*, a change of heart, and *pistis*, belief or trust. In the dynamic of the dialogue which is thus begun, the two are closely related, if not actually the same act. One is invited to believe that the word is indeed a revelation about the divinity. But such a response is not to something that is obvious, it is to the things that need to be "revealed" and "pointed out" precisely because they are not clear to the naked eye. That is the work of the prophet, the one who, in the name of the deity, provides the interpretation of events. It is the work of the visionary/dreamer who claims to be a kind of broker between the world of God and that of God's creation.[6] It is this claim of brokerage, proffered as it was by those who had no formal recognition in that role within society, which caused the conflict that surrounded both John and Jesus throughout their careers.[7] What Mark is telling his audience is that it took "belief" on the part of his contemporaries to accept that John and Jesus had legitimately fulfilled that role, that what they said was from God, and that to come to that act of belief they first had to undergo repentance.

Unfortunately, we too often understand repentance simply as a donning of sackcloth and ashes, an act of humiliation and self-accusation. It may indeed imply such things, but as we have seen, there is much more to it than that. Jesus preaches repentance and belief in a gospel which he himself had formally accepted at his own baptism. As we have seen in our discussion of the Baptist's preaching, repentance implies first of all an opening up, a seeing of things from another perspective from the one which up to now had ruled a person's life. It was a challenge to "come to one's senses" so that the vision presented by the preacher becomes the accepted vision of the convert, a vision by which he or she would, from that moment on, guide their "being" in community. A call for people to "repent and believe" is a call to adopt the interpre-

[6] For a discussion of the role of both official and unofficial limit-breaking agents within a society see B. Malina, *Origins*, 143–154.

[7] The controversy surrounding limit-breaking agents has to do with a society's recognition of their competence to reverse or transform a person's social standing within the group, or, on a broader level, to proffer an alternate scenario for achieving the fulfillment of a group's ideals.

tation of reality which the preacher is proclaiming, to trust that this is indeed the correct path to achieving the goals which had been set out from the beginning in the name of the divinity and to which all striving is directed. It is an act of trust, and a rather radical one at that. For in its recognition of prophetic status and mission, it adheres to the divine sanction and authority of the prophet to "build up and to tear down." No mean claim this! If indeed it truly reflects the prophetic proclamation of Jesus, it is no wonder that he caused such a stir among his contemporaries, for his teaching was radically at odds with so much that had been accepted for so long. But if it reflects the proclamation of Jesus, it just as truly reflects his own experience with John, under whose aegis he underwent his own conversion and performed such a sign of repentance. As the Gospels tell it, it was only after his time with John that he was to come into Galilee proclaiming this gospel.

What, then, is the content of that gospel? It seems so different from the kerygma of the early Church preached by Paul, which centers on the saving death and resurrection of Christ. "The time is fulfilled, and the kingdom of God is at hand" (RSV). What a sense of finality this preaching implies! It leans on the prophetic notion of the ultimate fulfillment of the will of God in the time of God's good pleasure. It is the Day of the Lord, a day of justice and judgment, but a day also of wonder and amazement at what people see and behold! It is a notion that is often taken up in the challenges of the kingdom of God attributed to Jesus, and again in the text of Acts that we saw at the beginning of this chapter. One can only marvel at the artistry of Mark, who has used the missionary language of the Church to craft this summary of the teaching of Jesus![8] In doing so he is claiming an affinity between the teaching of his Church and the lifework of its Master. This, he is saying, is the meaning, and these the implications of the Life that he is about to unfold to them. It is as if he were making room for the hearers of the words of his book to be

---

[8] See R. Schnackenburg, "Das Evangelium im Verständnis des Ältesten Evangelisten," in: P. Hoffmann, et al., eds., *Orientierung an Jesus: Zur Theologie der Synoptiker* (Freiburg: Herder, 1973) 309–324; C. Kazmierski, *Jesus*, 15–18.

present there with the crowds in Galilee as Jesus proclaims his gospel, perhaps, however, with a little more insight than any of them might have had, had they been there at the time themselves. But he goes one step further, for at the very beginning of his work he traces the preaching of the gospel of Jesus as Christ and Son of God to the appearance of John in the desert, which, he makes clear, was "according to the Scriptures."[9]

This teaching, moreover, was couched in that same Isaianic call to repentance that was first uttered by the Baptist in the wilderness, the call of time fulfilled, of repentance, and of peace. But now Mark is attempting to explain the meaning of that image to a generation of believers who are far removed from the time and place of the ministry of John and of Jesus, a meaning which for them is so often only implied and sometimes even hidden in the comings and goings of John and Jesus and of those who took up their mantle.

It is as if the image itself is dominated by a kind of parousia, a final and magnificent visiting of the people by their Lord![10] But the announcement of such a parousia serves only as a preparation for the final dwelling of the King among his people. And so the kingdom is at hand where those who see and hear this prophetic word in the person of the Messiah together form a coalition of believers. John had indeed prepared the way with his vision of the kingdom. The oracles of Isaiah which gave legitimacy to his ministry were again proclaimed in that of Jesus and of the community which adhered to him as their Lord.

Visions of Violence

Prophets are not the only ones who have visions and dreams. And it is often the clash of dreams which leads to discord within a community.

We have already seen how the tradition had preserved a memory of Jesus' high regard for John and his work. One of these traditions, which was to be adopted by both Matthew and Luke, has obviously been used and reworked a number of times, even before the evangelists fit it into the framework

[9] C. Kazmierski, *Jesus*, 18–21.
[10] A. Oepke, in *Theological Dictionary of the New Testament* 5: 858–871.

of their own Gospels. It is the challenging saying about enter-
ing the kingdom through violence. "From the days of John
the Baptist until now the kingdom of heaven has suffered violence, and men of violence take it by force" (Matt 11:12 RSV).
The Lukan form of the saying is quite different from that found
in Matthew,[11] but in both cases it is coupled with a saying about
the Prophets and the Law. "For all the prophets and the Law
prophesied until John," says Matthew, "and if you are willing to accept it, he is Elijah who is to come" (vv. 13-14 RSV).

It is notoriously difficult to reconstruct the original form of
this saying or to place it within a specific context in the life
of Jesus, for it is clear that both of the evangelists have radically adapted the tradition that they had received. Now, the
possibilities of interpretation are, in a sense, overwhelming.[12]
Consequently, there have been many attempts at situating the
saying within the ministry of Jesus that bear close scrutiny.
We cannot do that here. What is important, however, is that
the majority of these attempts at reconstruction respect the
authenticity of the saying and the fact that it traces the "beginning of the kingdom" to John the Baptist.[13] Moreover, what
also seems to be certain is that in one way or another, the kingdom of God was described as being assaulted or hindered by
violence![14] What is this connection between John, the kingdom,
and violence?

In chapter 21 of Matthew's Gospel, Jesus tells a parable about
two sons. The setting for the dialogue which the evangelist

[11] "The law and the prophets were until John; since then the good news
of the kingdom of God is preached, and everyone enters it violently"
(Luke 16:16).

[12] See the discussion in P. S. Cameron, *Violence and the Kingdom: The
Interpretation of Matthew 11:12* (Frankfurt: Peter Lang, 1984).

[13] N. Perrin (*Rediscovering the Teaching of Jesus* [New York: Harper and
Row, 1967] 75-76) summarizes the reasons for this, but gives a slightly
different interpretation from that proposed here. For the view against
authenticity see P. Hoffmann, *Studien zur Theologie der Logienquelle*,
Münster: Aschendorff, 1972) 60-70. H. Merklein (*Die Gottesherrschaft als
Handlugsprinzip. Untersuchung zur Ethik Jesu* [Würzburg: Echter, 1978] 85-
87) argues against the position that the kingdom is in relation to John.

[14] J. Ernst (*Johannes der Täufer*, 70), suggests that this might perhaps refer
to John's death.

narrates is Jerusalem, within the precincts of the Temple, where Jesus had just faced a confrontation with the chief priests and elders of the people. "By what authority are you doing these things," they had asked, "and who gave you this authority?" (RSV). Jesus had confounded their confrontation by challenging them to make a public declaration about the baptism of John. Was it from God, or was it a merely human affair? Now he goes one step further in his countercharge with this parable, the first in a series of three (The Two Sons, The Wicked Husbandmen, and the Great Supper) which progressively charge his opponents with infidelity and warn of their ultimate rejection by God. The chapter is a wonderful example of the challenge-riposte dynamic in the context of the struggle for status and legitimacy. The most important element in the exchange, moreover, is the audience, however silent it may be, since they, in the long run, are the ones who grant status.

"What do you think," Jesus asks,

> "A man had two sons; and he went to the first and said, 'Son, go and work in the vineyard today.' And he answered, 'I will not'; but afterward he repented and went. And he went to the second and said the same; and he answered, 'I go, sir,' but did not go. Which of the two did the will of his father?" (RSV).

Unlike the refusal to answer that ended the challenge about the baptism of John, the opponents of Jesus here give an answer: "The first one."

From the looks of things, the answer that the priests and elders gave to Jesus was the right one! There was no question about it. The first son was the one who, in fact, fulfilled the will of his father, even though it was his brother who had promised to do so. The parable itself is a story about the difference between saying and doing, about one who seems to be a rebellious son, but in fact does the will of the father, while the other, who is faithful in word, is in fact shown to be a liar in deed. In contemporary terms one might say it is a parable about "putting your money where your mouth is!"

But Matthew wishes to draw a further lesson from this story, and to that purpose adds a saying of Jesus which calls to mind the dynamic encounter which underlies the striking story of Nathan and David in 2 Samuel 12.

"Judge this case for me!" says Nathan.

> "In a certain town there were two men, one rich, the other poor. The rich man had flocks and herds in great numbers. But the poor man had nothing at all except one little ewe lamb that he had bought. He nourished her, and she grew up with him and his children. She shared the little food he had and drank from his cup and slept in his bosom. She was like a daughter to him. Now, the rich man received a visitor, but he would not take from his own flocks and herds to prepare a meal for the wayfarer who had come to him. Instead he took the poor man's ewe lamb and made a meal of it for his visitor" (NAB).

As all parables, this one is meant to incite a passionate reaction, and David responds to the story with great anger and indignation. The man merits death, he says, and because he has had no pity, he must make fourfold restitution! But Nathan, with all the authority that a prophet can muster, dramatically replies to him, "You are the man!"

As a result of this encounter between prophet and king, David repents in sackcloth and fasting. What Matthew wishes to portray in his narrative, however, is just the opposite. Again the leaders of the people are confronted by a prophetic challenge. But this time there is no repentance! "Truly I say to you," answers Jesus, "the tax collectors and the harlots go into the kingdom before you!"

> For John came to you in the way of righteousness, and you did not believe him, but the tax collectors and harlots believed him; and even when you saw it, you did not afterward repent and believe him" (RSV).

In the eyes of Jesus, John had been their Nathan. Not only did they not pay heed to his judgment, but they failed to respond to what Matthew sees as a sign of his righteousness: the conversion of tax collectors and harlots, people who, in the nature of things, were beyond the pale of forgiveness. In the end, the chief priests and Pharisees realized that he was speaking about them, but their reaction was not repentance but rather an attempt to have him arrested (Matt 21:45-46).

The response of Jesus which Matthew has added to the parable of the Two Sons, is, in all probability, a saying that was originally independent of its present context. (It appears in Luke 7:29-30 in a slightly different form, but in an altogether different setting.) Many exegetes judge that the different forms which the words of Jesus take in Matthew and Luke are both developments of a Q saying which ultimately does go back to Jesus himself. Others feel, however, that Matthew has composed the saying himself, on the basis of the tradition that John, who was so widely admired by the populace at large, was in turn rejected by the elite sectors of society.[15] In either case, however, the tradition would have, in fact, handed down the substance of the case.

What is at issue, however, is just this basic tradition about John and its relationship to Jesus and his ministry.[16] "The tax collectors and harlots believed him," those who, almost by definition, had been excluded from the covenant community. These were the ones who were to become so central to the ministry of Jesus. Even to approach them with the hope of salvation was to cut at the very heart of contemporary piety, and especially of the doctrine of the Pharisees. What is important here is that Matthew feels free to use this saying about John in the way he does. He can presume that his audience will indeed relate to the connections he has made and finally give the grant of honor in this confrontation to Jesus and not to the Pharisees.

On his part, Jesus was to approach those very people with the challenging parable of his first beatitude: "Blessed are you poor, for yours is the kingdom of God!"[17] (RSV). For tax col-

---

[15] R. Gardner, *Jesus' Appraisal*, 180–181; J. Fitzmyer, *Luke* I, 671.

[16] Is it possible that Matthew has in this text simply taken an element of the ministry of Jesus and pushed it back, as it were, into the ministry of John. After all, the First Gospel has been shown to exhibit an "artfully developed parallelism" between John and Jesus. The question is whether or not it is at least as probable, or perhaps even more probable that his clear and "daring assimilation" of John to Jesus is, in fact, based within the memory of his Church.

[17] Luke 6:20, parallel Matthew 5:3. Luke's use of the second person "you" is generally seen as more authentic than Matthew's "Blessed are the poor in spirit."

lectors and harlots to be able to be addressed in this way was, in the mind of Jesus, cause for celebration within the kingdom. And so the tradition again and again presents him as sitting at table with just such as these! What Matthew is presenting here, however, is not the joy over such a gospel, but the lack of it. John had opened the doors of the kingdom to those who were shut out. But the priests and elders of the story were not moved to a change of heart by this wonderful sight. For them it was not the "good news of the kingdom," but bad news. "Even when you saw it, you did not afterward repent and believe in him" (RSV). It is for this reason, Jesus says, that the tax collectors and harlots will go through those doors and into the kingdom, while the leaders will be shut out. They had seen and listened, but had not understood. There was no repentance!

It is against the background of this saying of Jesus that we now must understand the saying concerning John and the violence of the kingdom. F. W. Danker has proposed the view[18] that this saying originally arose as a complaint by the Pharisees against John the Baptist. "Since the appearance of the Baptist," they would have charged, "until the present moment, the kingdom of God is being violently assaulted and violent men wish to rob it!"[19] In other words, John's baptism and preaching had done violence to their vision of the kingdom and could not be tolerated by any true member of God's people! The kingdom is not for tax collectors and harlots! It is for the pious of Israel! Surely these would be the words of those whose visions and dreams were different from those of John. On his part, Jesus was to turn these very sentiments against them and use them as a testimony to John's success, tearing at the very heart of their reality and arousing their bitter resentment.

The Death of Prophets and Visionaries

According to Josephus, it was the popularity of John that was ultimately to be his undoing. He was arrested and finally

---

[18] "Luke 16:16—An Opposition Logion," *Journal of Biblical Literature* 77 (1958) 231-243. Against this see Gardner, *Jesus' Appraisal*, 238, n. 17.

[19] As reconstructed by W. G. Kümmel, cited in Wink, *John the Baptist*, 21.

executed by Antipas, one of the sons of Herod the Great, under whose family Rome ruled Jewish Palestine from 37 B.C. to A.D. 70.

From the point of view of the elite sector of society, to speak the language of kingdom was to enter into the dialogue of politics. But this was a dialogue that was carefully boundaried. It was not the ground for peasants to tread! "Herod had him put to death," says Josephus, though he was a good man and had exhorted the Jews to lead righteous lives."[20] But such righteousness was not Herod's concern. Or perhaps it was! "When others too joined the crowds about him, because they were aroused to the highest degree by his sermons, Herod became alarmed" (*Antiquities* 18.5.2 no. 118).

The status of the Jewish elite was precarious as it was, without the threatened fire that a revolutionary movement such as John's could enkindle. Josephus continues, "Eloquence that had so great an effect on mankind might lead to some sort of sedition, for it looked as if they would be guided by John in everything they did" (see n. 20 above). If anything, this witness of Josephus supports the picture of John's popularity among the Jews that Matthew had built upon in chapter 11 of his Gospel, and now (as opposed to Mark) provides as the motivation for his execution. "What did you go out into the desert to see?" John was a prophet, the greatest of them all. "Herod decided, therefore," concludes Josephus, "that it would be much better to strike first and be rid of him before his work led to an uprising, than to wait for an upheaval, get involved in a difficult situation, and see his mistake."[21]

The times indeed were tense. For a ruler who himself was walking on a tightrope, such a caution—some would call it paranoia—might appear as virtue. That it did little to help Antipas either in maintaining his throne, or the affection of his people, is one of the hard-learned lessons of the tyrant.

Within the New Testament, Luke (3:19-20) gives only the briefest notice of Herod's responsibility for the arrest of John,

---

[20] *The Antiquities of the Jews* 18.5.2 [nos. 116–119]).

[21] E. Rivkin (*What Crucified Jesus?* Nashville: Abingdon, 1984), discusses this in connection with the death of Jesus and concludes that it was the precarious position of the Romans that was at stake.

which he places immediately after a summary of his preaching. Matthew (14:3-12) and Mark (6:14-29), on the other hand, narrate the story about the beheading of John at great length. The story in Mark is more elaborate than Matthew's, but Matthew tells us that, after they buried him, the disciples of John came to bring the news to Jesus. Both evangelists, however, are concerned to present his death within the context of prophetic outrage at the illegal marriage of the king. Thus John becomes the defender of Torah and a champion of the righteousness of the kingdom. Yet there is a reticence to blame Herod, for in both cases, (but more so in Mark than in Matthew) it is not Herod who is blamed, but his wife Herodias,[22] who contrives and succeeds in forcing the king, in his honor, to put John to death. In fact, as Mark would have it, Herod "felt the attraction of his (John's) words . . . yet because of his oath and the presence of the guests" (Mark 6:20, 26 NAB), he does not refuse.[23] The cunning manipulation of Herodias including the compliance of her daughter, is an interesting example of the machinations which abound in an agonistic society in which women are given short shrift. Herodias would have lost everything had John's influence on Antipas proved true. As it was in the end, she and she alone came out the winner.

But we cannot end our discussion here. There is another text which we must examine, for it too speaks of John's death. It is a text in which the image of John as Elijah comes into play. In Matthew 17:10-13 (parallel Mark 9:11-13) the disciples ask Jesus about the scribal teaching that "Elijah must come first." The context provided by the evangelists is the descent from the mount of Transfiguration, where the three chosen disciples, Peter, James, and John, had just witnessed the glorification of Jesus in the presence of Moses and Elijah and had heard the voice from heaven proclaim him as "Beloved Son." Following on the confession of Peter with its striking contrast to what

---

[22] Luke's omission (Luke 3:19) of the name of Philip is perhaps due to the fact that Antipas' half-brother was married not to Herodias, as Mark would have it, but to her daughter Salome. For a discussion of the problems involved see W. Shenk, "Gefangenschaft," 464–470; J. Ernst, *Johannes der Täufer,* 341.

"people were saying," this narrative has now removed any confusion about Jesus' role. But the disciples are ordered to tell no one what they had seen "until the Son of Man be raised from the dead." At this point Mark adds an explanatory note that has been omitted by Matthew. "They kept all this to themselves," he states, "but continued to discuss what 'to rise from the dead' meant."

The question about Elijah follows this: "Why do the Scribes say," they ask, "that Elijah must come first?" The question has to do with the divine necessity of Elijah's appearance, and for this reason, in Mark, where this is a constant concern of the evangelist, Jesus must answer with a reference to Scripture. From the immediate context, however, it would seem that the coming of Elijah is somehow connected with the resurrection of the dead.[24] For these disciples the "teaching of the Scribes" about Elijah now presents a great problem, for they had just experienced his presence, seemingly unconnected with any end-time resurrection. The answer of Jesus to this dilemma is basically the same in both Matthew and Mark, except that Matthew has rearranged the order of Jesus' words, perhaps in the interest of clarity, and made some slight additions which seem to take the sting out of Jesus' charge.[25] But the three main points to Jesus' answer are constant. First, Elijah does come (first); his role is "to restore all things." The stress in this part of Jesus' answer is not on the sign value of his coming vis-à-vis the end of time, but on the content of his mission of restoration which Malachi had described as "turning the hearts of the fathers to their children, and the hearts of the children to their fathers" (Mal 3:24 RSV). In Sirach 48:10 this mission is presented even more clearly as a work of restoration. "You are destined, it is written, in time to come to put an end to wrath before the day of the LORD, to turn back

[23] See also D. A. Black, "The Text of Mark 6.20," *New Testament Studies* 34 (1988) 141–145.

[24] See Revelation 11:4-15, where the Moses and Elijah traditions of Judaism stand behind the prophetic witnesses who give testimony and are slain by the beast.

[25] In 17:12 (RSV), Matthew adds "they did not know him" in reference to the rejection of Elijah!

the hearts of fathers toward their sons, and to re-establish the tribes of Jacob'' (NAB).

The second point of Jesus' answer is that this Elijah has come already, but not only has he come, he has been rejected by his people. Thus, the restoration has not taken place. Finally, the third point to Jesus' answer is that this rejection is paradigmatic of what the Son of Man must undergo. The pattern that is presented, then, is a paralleling of the fate of those who are sent by God as prophets of the work of restoration; Elijah, the second Elijah who has already come, and this Son of Man.

Perhaps it would be interesting to examine the Markan form of the narrative a little more closely. ''Elijah does come,'' answers Jesus, ''to restore all things.'' But then, ''how is it that it is written in the Scriptures that the Son of Man must suffer many things and be treated with contempt?''[26] There are two questions here, one about the coming of Elijah, referred to as the ''teaching of the Scribes,'' and the other, posed by Jesus, concerning the Son of Man, referred to as scriptural teaching, a teaching which Mark had already introduced in 8:31.

In form, the passage is much like Mark 12:35-37 (RSV):

> ''How can the scribes say that the Christ is the son of David?
> David himself, inspired by the Holy Spirit, declared
> > 'The Lord said to my Lord,
> > Sit at my right hand
> > till I put thy enemies under thy feet.'
> David himself calls him Lord; so how is he his son?''

The teaching of the scribes (How can the scribes say . . .) is challenged by a teaching from the Scripture (David . . . inspired by the Holy Spirit . . .). In this text, Jesus does not give an answer but only presents the dilemma to challenge his hearers to come to grips with the problem. In fact, he does not deny the teaching of the scribes, but respects it for what it is. The implication is that yes, the Messiah is David's son, just

---

[26] One has difficulty agreeing with the deus ex machina-like solution of Wink (*John the Baptist*, 14–15) that this son of man saying was originally a reference to Elijah. As to the Scripture allusion, dare one suggest the Suffering Servant of Isaiah as the paradigmatic of the ''suffering prophet'' (Jeremiah)?

as in Mark 9:12 Jesus affirms that Elijah does come. But notice that in this text, although Jesus does not give an answer which resolves the dilemma, for the Christian reader of the text it is clear: The Messiah is Son of David, but he is also Son of God and therefore David's Lord.[27] In Mark 9:11-13, however, Jesus does answer the dilemma: "I tell you, Elijah has come and they did to him whatever they pleased, as it is written of him" (RSV).[28]

All this has led to many questions about the authenticity of the tradition reflected in Mark 9:11-13. Indeed the best arguments have long seemed to be on the side of those who suggest that it took shape within the Christian community, and even that verse 13, the saying about the rejection of Elijah, took shape in the study of the evangelist.[29]

But we must pursue our questioning a little further. The relation of the imagery in this passage with that in Matthew 11:7-11, which we discussed earlier, is quite clear. John is (like) Elijah! And their likeness is in the role that each plays in the plan of God. This is made clear, for in both cases, "it has been written of him!" But what of Mark 9:13, a text which is really unique in that it speaks of a rejected Elijah, a very different notion than that associated with the Elijah of Malachi 3:1, which stands behind the disciples' question. The question must be asked: Is this notion of a rejected Elijah likely to have developed from the Malachi pattern? It does not seem so. Is it necessary, then, to say that the evangelist has conceived it in his own workshop, so to speak?

It must be noted that the controlling motif of verse 13 is not suffering, but rejection. Not an unusual experience among the Prophets! If anything, the tradition is clear that this was indeed the experience of John. Why then must we deny this text the note of authenticity? John was considered a prophet, as Elijah was. And indeed, John was rejected by the rulers of

[27] This is very close to the "theology" of Romans 1:3-4 and is central to Mark's conception of Jesus; see below, chapter 5.

[28] Matthew 17:12-13 omits the reference to Scripture here and clarifies the reference to Elijah/John lest there should be any question as to its application.

[29] See J. Ernst, *Johannes der Täufer*, 30-34.

Israel, as Elijah himself was.[30] To deny this insight to Jesus and the followers of John on principles of redaction criticism is pushing methodological purity beyond the bounds of common sense. Without this basic understanding of the John-Elijah comparison, the entire further development of the motif of John/Elijah as the precursor of the end-time Messiah makes no sense. For it has been clearly shown that within contemporary Judaism, there was no such pattern at all which could provide such a model.[31]

Such a scenario would suggest then, that among his contemporaries, there was a pattern of comparison which simply would have likened John to Elijah (the prophet from of old) who haunted the desert places and became the "troubler of Israel." It would have been applied to John by his own supporters in the context of the challenge-riposte dynamic set in motion by his own referral to Isaiah 40:3 to justify his desert ministry. In other words, in reference to the texts which use the Elijah image, we would suggest that while it may be that none of the texts as they stand represent the exact words of Jesus, there stands behind them the unmistakable imprint of a very early use of the Elijah imagery in reference to John.[32] What did they go out into the desert to see? A prophet, indeed a very great prophet, a prophet like Elijah was. A perfect image indeed, and one that was to prove fruitful in itself for the further development that would be necessary in the ongoing life of the movement even after the death of John and Jesus.

"Elijah has come and they have done to him whatever they pleased!"—a prophetic troubler of Israel who had been rejected

[30] Cf. 1 Kings 19. It is not necessary therefore to search for Scriptures about a suffering Elijah, or to describe Mark's reference to Scripture as mistaken and confused as does, e.g., Wink, *John the Baptist*, 13–17.

[31] See M. Faierstein, "Why Do the Scribes Say That Elijah Must Come First?" *Journal of Biblical Literature* 100 (1981) 75–86; J. Fitzmyer, "More About Elijah Coming First," *Journal of Biblical Literature* 104 (1985) 295–296. Contemporary Judaism did, however, provide a pattern of the martyred Elijah (see R. Pesch, *Markusevangelium II*, 80–81).

[32] The tradition that the Elijah image was also used of Jesus (Mark 8:27-28 parallel; Mark 6:14-16 parallel) opens up another avenue of questioning that cannot be entered into at this point.

by his own people. If there is little reason to look elsewhere than to Jesus and/or his contemporaries for the origin of this comparison, then he was using an image which speaks of the people's rejection of the prophets, with roots deep in the reform tradition of Israel. The prophet Jeremiah uses this same image and seems almost to suggest that theirs is to be read as a history of damnation, for the nation had continuously rejected those sent by God.

> From the day that your fathers came out of the land of Egypt to this day, I have persistently sent all my servants the prophets to them, day after day; and yet, they did not listen to me, or incline their ear, but stiffened their neck. They did worse than their fathers! (Jer 7:25-26 RSV).

Indeed, they were,

> . . . a foolish and senseless people,
> . . . who have eyes but see not,
> who have ears, but hear not (Jer 5:21 RSV).

That such patterns were available to image the reality of Israel's dealings with its prophets is evidenced in the parable of the Wicked Vinedressers (Mark 12:1-10), which many scholars readily attribute to Jesus. As we have it now, it too is marked by Christian reflection. After all, it is an allegory, a form open to expansion by its very nature. But at the base of the present text lies the unmistakable modeling on the parable in Isaiah 5:1-7 coupled with that prophetic motif of the rejection of the prophets that we have already seen so graphically spelled out in Jeremiah.[33] It is a parable fraught with political significance since it is clearly directed against the leaders of the people, whose false stewardship is said to lead to ultimate disaster. How like so many of Jesus' parables!

It is interesting to see how the same motif is taken up by Luke and woven into the speech of Stephen in Acts 7:

---

[33] J. Blank, ''Die Sendung des Sohnes. Zur christologischen Bedeutung des Gleichnisses von den bösen Winzern,'' *Neues Testament und Kirche,* ed. J. Gnilka (Freiburg: Herder, 1974) 11–41; C. Kazmierski, *Jesus,* 127–136.

You stiff-necked people, uncircumcised in heart and ears, you always
resist the Holy Spirit.
As your fathers did, so do you.
Which of the prophets did not your fathers persecute?
And they killed those who announced beforehand the coming of the Righteous One, whom you have now betrayed and murdered . . . (Acts 7:51-53 RSV).

These are strong words indeed, and fraught with terrible consequences, but they are, in fact, reminiscent of the very words of the prophets themselves that were part and parcel of the language of accusation among rivaling groups within the community. Worthy are they, indeed, of continued reflection. We must return to them in chapter 6.

Jesus and the Death of John

Often the safeguards that a discipline sets for itself become counterproductive in that they may inhibit scholars from pursuing lines of thought that are not clearly stated in the texts. The so-called criterion of dissimilarity[34] has been a powerful tool in discerning the uniqueness of certain elements of Jesus' teaching, but it has at the same time become a straitjacket which limits even where logic tells us that freedom should prevail. Such, it seems to me, has been the case in the entire discussion about the origins of the early Christian doctrines concerned with the death of Jesus.

It is inconceivable that a man in Jesus' shoes would not reflect on death, his own in particular, given his career and his experience with the death of John. Mark 9:9-13 alone points in that direction, however obliquely. Without entering into the controversy, I would dare at this point to suggest that John's death did indeed set in motion that reflection within the Jesus movement which was ultimately to result in the use of Jewish patterns of martyrdom and substitutionary theology to describe the death of Jesus. The passion predictions (Mark 8:31; 9:31;

[34] The criterion of dissimilarity would hold that a saying might be attributed to Jesus only if there were no parallels in contemporary Judaism or primitive Christianity.

10:33-34 parallel), the saying in Mark 10:45 about the Son of Man giving his life as a "ransom for many," and the words of Jesus at the Last Supper (Mark 14:22-25 parallel; 1 Cor 11:23-26), were not cut from new cloth and, as it were, after the fact. The groundwork for their ultimate development after the death and resurrection of Jesus was laid with great care during the ongoing dynamics of his own ministry. The relationship of Jesus and his followers to John the Baptist played no small role in this. In the least instance, if Jesus had considered John as a prophet of extraordinary stature, then his death must have signaled a warning note. "What is happening here?" "Where is God now that God's servant is being persecuted?" "My God, My God, why have you abandoned me?" These are questions that our experience often forces on us. The Jews of Jesus' time had a tradition of reflection on those questions from which to draw in circumstances such as these. There is no reason to doubt that, as the texts suggest, Jesus, together with his followers, did just that!

Summary

Dreams and visions are the stuff of prophecy. They reflect a judgment of things that comes from the outside, often from a perspective quite different and even in contradiction to what has been generally accepted in a society. As we continue our journey in search of John, we are invited not only to understand his vision and how different it perhaps was from that of the majority of his contemporaries, but also to enter into the discourse that this vision provoked among them. John called for a conversion that was an invitation to mold a new communal reality in which all of Israel understood its need for forgiveness and at the same time the universal availability of God's grace. Such a vision was a challenge not only to the elite sectors of society but to the exclusivism of the various (customary) "ways" of Israel that might provide alternative patterns of Torah observance to the already discredited proponents of the Great (official) Tradition. It was thus political as well as personal since it implied a new structuring of reality whose social, economic, and religious dimensions would set John and his followers against the traditional authority in both

the political and domestic systems. It is not surprising therefore that his activity provoked not only the charge of violence,
but violence itself. It was the way of the prophets—and their
destiny.

"Elijah had already come, and they did to him what they
wanted."

5

In the Age of the Messiah

One of the underlying assumptions of this book has been that the complexity of the tradition about John the Baptist reflects a development brought about by the dynamics of acceptance and rejection in a society where honor and shame were pivotal values of social intercourse. We have used labeling theory as a model to help us unravel some of that complexity and have concluded that the roots of the New Testament's presentation of John as a prophet lie deep within the memory of his followers. Developed in an attempt to maintain and increase his honor amid countering pressures to diminish his position in the eyes of his contemporaries, John had been labeled a "voice in the wilderness," and likened to Elijah, the great troubler of Israel. Such affirmations of prominence made during his lifetime served not only to maintain his position in the eyes of his followers but allowed for the continuance of his ministry among the people. Furthermore, it was these images and comparisons which were to provide the raw materials with which the early Christians were to build as they, in their turn, attempted to situate him within their own worldview.

While we have already discussed much of the tradition from this perspective, it is important that we now consider the social changes that prompted these reevaluations on the part of the early Christians. Most important, of course, is the fact that it was now not only John, but Jesus too who had been executed by the political authorities. His sentence had been passed and carried out by the Romans under pressure from the Jerusalem elite, who, according to the tradition, were able to rally considerable support in Jerusalem. But the changes did not end there, for now his followers proceeded to acclaim him as Son of God and Savior.

Contemporary scholarship recognizes this post-Easter acclamation as the dawn of the Church's messianic consciousness regarding Jesus. Yet, in so far as the Church proclaimed his Messiahship, it had to give that title a new content in order to make possible its application to their Master, who, for all intents and purposes, had nothing in his history to recommend him for any of its contemporary expectations, to say nothing of the royal acclamation which they were to adopt. And so the inevitability of tension with the past, of conflict, and of the need for further legitimation, presented themselves anew. It now became vital for the movement to confront its newfound pronouncements about the position and function of Jesus with the strength of its memory of his ministry. In the course of things, this was to lead to a radical re-formation of its picture of Jesus and of his relationship to John the Baptist as well.

Your Prophets Are Dead

We ended the last chapter noting something of the situation caused by Herod's murder of John. If his execution was to cause such anxiety and disruption within the movement he began, the crucifixion of Jesus so soon afterward was to do no less. It was the perfect foil for any continued influence the two prophets might have had. In fact, one could expect that any notion of the "gathering of Israel" that might have marked their ministries would be abandoned.

But such was not to be the case.

There is a wonderful story at the end of St. Luke's Gospel (Luke 24:13-35) about two of the followers of Jesus who are on a journey to Emmaus,[1] a city not far from Jerusalem. It was on the first day of the week, the evangelist tells us, the third

---

[1] For the possibilities and difficulties in locating Emmaus, as well as the textual problems involved, see Fitzmyer, *Luke* II, 1561–1562.

after the death of their master, and they bore the burden of great sorrow and distress.

" 'We were hoping that he was to be the deliverer of Israel,' '' they tell the stranger who joins them on the road.

As they recount the events of those last days, the stranger makes a startling reply.

" 'How slow you are to believe,' '' he says,

"and," the evangelist continues, "he explained the Scriptures to them . . . that the Messiah had to suffer before entering into his glory."

After taking a meal with them, he vanishes from their sight.

The story ends on a striking note that resolves any conflict that may have remained in the overall narrative of chapter 24. Upon returning to Jerusalem, these followers of Jesus find that "the Eleven had gathered together with the others and were saying that the Lord has indeed been raised from the dead, and has appeared to Simon!"[2] Of course, by now the two are no longer skeptical or surprised, for they were able to explain "what had happened on the road, and how they had come to know him in the breaking of the bread" (v. 35). For these disciples, it was not the appearance of the risen Lord that brought them insight and understanding as it had to Simon, but the unfolding of the Scriptures and the breaking of the bread.

One may wonder what memories were awakened, what images evoked, as the early Christians heard this story in the midst of their communities? For Luke,[3] there is clearly an association to be made between this narrative, the story of the Last Supper (Luke 22:19) and the summary of the life of the Church that he provides in Acts 2:42.[4] For the generation of Luke's readers, faith in Jesus as the risen Savior and the experience of his presence among them was no longer to be

---

[2] Cf. 1 Corinthians 15:4-5 for what is probably the earliest record of this "statement of faith."

[3] It is generally agreed that this story has been artistically crafted by Luke and filled with theological motifs which he will pick up in the Acts of the Apostles. See Fitzmyer, *Luke* II, 1553–1572.

[4] See also Luke 9:10-17; Acts 20:7, 11; 27:35. Fitzmyer, *Luke* II, 1569.

found in vision and ecstasy, but in the Scriptures and in their celebration of Eucharist.[5]

Of course, as it stands now, the story is marked by an already well-developed theology: Jesus was indeed the deliverer of Israel. His suffering did not contradict his messianic status for it was "according to the Scriptures." For our purposes, however, it is not only the theology reflected in the narrative that is of importance, but also the background and dynamic which it reflects, for here we are able to discern the social context of much of early Christian liturgical and theological development. At the beginning of the narrative the disciples are presented as being crestfallen and distraught. Their master's death had thrown them into confusion. They were leaving Jerusalem. The implication is that the group which had been with Jesus was breaking up. Even the empty tomb and the angelic vision experienced by some of their number did not overcome their "slowness of faith."

Many years before Luke wrote his Gospel, the Apostle Paul had to face a situation which was quite similar to the one pictured here. The greatest obstacle to his preaching was the Cross of Jesus. It was a stumbling block, he wrote, a scandal to both Jew and Gentile alike. A generation later, the evangelist Mark was still struggling with the same problem, the solution to which he situates in the very ministry of Jesus. "It was by divine necessity that the Son of Man had to suffer and die," Jesus teaches his disciples (Mark 8:31).

Now it is true that both Paul and Mark were responding to tensions within their own communities, but these tensions were more widespread than it may appear. In fact, it would not be too much to say that for the earliest communities, the manner of Jesus' death presented a far greater challenge to the legitimacy of their preaching than Jesus' opponents ever had to his. If one believed in signs, here was one that needed little interpretation. Paul was able to cite a Scripture passage which laid it out rather clearly: "Cursed be the man who is hung on a tree" (Gal 3:13; Deut 21:23). How could one who had been so clearly rejected take his place among the prophets of Israel,

[5] According to Fitzmyer, *Luke* II, 1559, ". . . clearly Luke's way of referring to the Eucharist."

and his teaching find a place alongside their wisdom? They could not! And if what we have said about the relationship of Jesus to John is at all valid, then the repudiation of the one by his ignominious death on the cross would have fallen also to the other. No prophets these; their anointing was not attested by God's care in their greatest need. To this the Scriptures would attest.

But we must return to those disciples on the road to Emmaus. If their eyes had to be opened by the explanations of the stranger, it was because the Scriptures he used were not so evidently in place in the storehouse of Jewish apologetic. These were new Scriptures, or at least Scriptures that had been newly searched out and applied to a challenging situation at variance with the wisdom of the sages in opposition. It is for this reason that contemporary scholars can find no reference to suffering messiahs among the texts of Judaism, nor indeed any messianic notions that quite match those of the first Christian preachers. It was to the Christians' great credit that they were able to reinterpret the ancient texts and apply them with a freshness which was not unlike that used among the covenenters of Qumran. After all, the Scripture was the word of God, living and creative. It presupposed that each generation would take it up and infuse it with their own experience. How else was it to speak their language? It had always been so.

This, then, is the *Sitz im Leben* that form criticism has long spoken of, in this instance, the workshop of scriptural interpretation and communal celebration in which narratives such as these took their shape and were handed down. But that interpretation and celebration were situated within the context of the changing social position of the groups that were involved, as Jesus' movement experienced the shift from a broadly based political factionalism to the more boundaried existence of a kin-type group, seeking its own definition in a more hostile world. At the same time, the early Christian communities which were coming into being were as varied and diffuse as the Jewish parents from whom they were born. And so it should come as no surprise that the traditions they themselves developed would at times stand in tension with one another, and call for further dialogue and conciliation. At times the developments were influenced by patterns already adopted during the ministry of Jesus, now to be intensified in this new circumstance. Such were the stories about John the Baptist, the Elijah who had been rejected. If this was the pattern used by Jesus to make sense out of the death of his mentor, or even if we must finally attribute this patterning to the early Christians, then it stood at the threshold of the further developments which would unfold in the light of their joyous acclamations of his resurrection and his enthronement to messianic glory.

The Beginnings of Christian Eschatology

If it is clear that the death of Jesus became a major stumbling block for the acceptance of his message, it is just as clear that his disciples crafted their response as part of an overall search for legitimacy among an ever-expanding world of opposing groups within Judaism and in the Hellenistic world as well, where the focus of their attention soon shifted. That these responses took shape within the context of a struggle for honor and the concomitant role of Jesus and his group as brokers of divine favor suggests an aggressivity that has not often been recognized in these texts. To call these developments "politically motivated theology" is to cast no aspersion on the doctrines which were developed in this context, but rather to emphasize the essential link between the emerging structures of belief and the tensions which the group encountered in its struggle for honor, legitimation, and consolidation.

As we have suggested, it would seem that the earliest images and patterns adopted by the Christians in service of this labeling process were used to explain the death of Jesus as being somehow a part of God's plan, and thus to legitimate his teaching and prophetic status in the wake of his execution. This can be seen, at least partially, in certain strands of the primitive narration of the passion and death of Jesus, which have been shown to be replete with allusions to Scripture and sectarian patterns of reflection on the suffering endured by the righteous.[6] Whatever the relation of these traditions to one

---

[6] For a good summary of contemporary approaches to this see Hans-Reudi Weber, *The Cross: Tradition and Interpretation* (London: S.P.C.K., 1979).

another and to those of the death of the Baptist, their primitive nature attests to the effort which was made to rescue the honor of Jesus, his teaching, and the position of his followers in the wake of the overwhelming evidence to the contrary which the prevailing milieu provided.

The story of the disciples on the road to Emmaus, moreover, provides insight into a further development. In the exchange between the stranger and the two disciples, the focus is on the possibility that Jesus was the Messiah who could have brought deliverance to Israel. The image is clearly that of Davidic messianism. The concern of the disciples is that now that he is dead, Jesus cannot be this Messiah! Although closely related to each other, there is at least a logical separation between this and the Cross theology of the earliest traditions. Here we are concerned with an already qualified understanding of messiahship which goes much beyond the prophetic legitimation of the earlier texts. It is important to note the difference between the context reflected in each, even if we may not be able to assign any priority or focus of origin for the one or the other. At the same time, both are concerned with the legitimation of the person of Jesus and of his teaching in the light of evidence to the contrary. In this contest for honor, the position of the community is as much involved in that they are challenged to develop patterns of acclamation and affirmations of prominence which would be in continuity with their own history as well as sensitive to the demands of the surrounding culture. In other words, a dialogue was necessary in which each participant would be able at least to understand and relate to what the other is saying.

The earliest formulations of this latter labeling process are difficult to specify, but it might be helpful to stay with Luke and examine the pattern which he provides in the second chapter of the Book of Acts. Here Luke describes a series of events that are said to have taken place in Jerusalem on the Jewish feast of Pentecost which followed the death and resurrection of Jesus. With a staging that has been beautifully crafted, Luke has Peter confront a great crowd of Jews from every nation who had been thrown into confusion when they heard the ecstatic prayer of the Spirit-filled disciples. Referring to the prophet Joel and his oracle about the last days, Peter rehearses the events surrounding the death of Jesus and rushes into the climactic statement about his messiahship: "Therefore let the whole of Israel know beyond any doubt," he says, "that God has made both Lord and Messiah this Jesus whom you crucified" (Acts 2:36 NAB).

There has long been a lively discussion about the authenticity of the various speeches in Acts. The most radical position would argue that they are not authentic at all, but rather completely the composition of the evangelist, who reflects not the words of Peter on that occasion, nor indeed even the thinking of the primitive Church, but rather the theology of his own generation at the end of the first Christian century.[7] For others, the solution is a bit more nuanced, for while they would agree that the speeches in Acts are the composition of the author, they would argue that he has not created them from whole cloth, but rather has crafted them from older traditions which indeed reflect the kerygmatic formulations of the earliest communities.[8] This is verified, they argue, when one compares the content of these speeches with the content of the early kerygmatic formulae which have been isolated in other parts of the New Testament, most notably, the letters of Paul.

It is not necessary for us to enter the discussion at any length. The important point for our purposes is that in this tradition, Jesus is said to have become Messiah at, or in respect of, his resurrection from the dead. The implication is that he was not Messiah before this, at least not in the functional sense that is proclaimed in this layer of the tradition. One finds a parallel formulation in Romans 1:3-4,[9] in the tradition that Paul uses to show his readers in Rome his own adherence to the early kerygma which is central to their own belief. His preaching of the gospel, he tells them, is about God's Son:

---

[7] E. Haenchen, *Die Apostelgeschichte* (Göttingen: Vandenhoeck & Ruprecht, sixth edition; 1968) 139–152.

[8] C. H. Dodd, *The Apostolic Preaching and its Developments* (London: Hodder Stoughton, 1936) is the classic in this regard.

[9] See M. E. Boismard, "Constitue Fils de Dieu," *Revue Biblique* 60 (1953) 5–14; E. Linnemann, "Tradition und Interpretation in Rom 1, 3f," *Evangelische Theologie* 31 (1971) 264–276.

who was descended from David
according to the flesh
but was made Son of God in power
according to the spirit of holiness,
by his resurrection from the dead . . . (NAB).

The primitive nature of this tradition and its acceptance by both the Roman Church and Paul show how early this pattern gained predominance among the early preachers. Here is an actualization of the Davidic psalms of enthronement (Ps 2:7; 110:1). Thus the model that wins acceptance is that of the Royal Messiah: son of David, yes, but now anointed Son of God at his resurrection and able to send God's Spirit upon his people. The predominant messianic confessions of the Gospels are grounded in these post-Easter professions of faith that are now projected into the biography of Jesus. In the service of the proclamation, his ministry is now seen in terms altogether different than the original disciples could have even imagined. In any event, it is because of this post-Easter acclamation of Jesus' royal messianic status that the group was forced to struggle anew with the question of the Baptist's authority, his relationship to Jesus, and the relationship of both to the enigmatic figure of Elijah who played such a significant role in the dynamics of rejection and acceptance that marked both their ministries. The struggle was to find its resolution in an expansion of the very models provided during those ministries.

The Many Faces of Elijah

In first-century Judaism, the prophet Elijah seems to have been the patron saint of many causes.[10] Most of the legend that surrounded his figure was rooted in the Scriptures, but there remains some difficulty in our ability to distinguish the traditions that predate, from those that follow the New Testament period. Elijah the miracle worker, Elijah the messiah, and even Elijah as a helper in time of need, have all been recognized as playing a role in various New Testament texts.[11] The dan-

[10] See G. Molin, "Elijahu der Prophet und sein Weiterleben in den Hoffnungen des Judentums und Christenheit," *Judaica* 8 (1952) 65–94.

[11] See, e.g., J. Jeremias, "Elias," in *Theological Dictionary of the New Testament* 2: 934–941.

ger is that one can easily read the complex of these in the light of later traditions and thus mistake the import that they have in a particular place in the Christian tradition. This is particularly true in those which were used to spell out the relationship between Jesus and John the Baptist.

We have already discussed some aspects of those difficulties in chapter 3. We must now return briefly to one of those texts that formed the basis of our remarks. It is the scriptural citation which is first found in the "Q" tradition as the center of Jesus' address to the crowds concerning John.

> "This is he of whom it is written,
>> 'Behold, I send my messenger before your face,
>> who shall prepare your way before you.' "

It is clear that in its present form, the speaker within the citation is Yahweh. What is not so clear, however, is the one to whom Yahweh is speaking. To find the answer therefore, one must turn to the context, first of all that from which the text was taken, and then that in which it is used.

For most exegetes the answer provided by such an examination would point to the Messiah as the recipient of Yahweh's promise. This interpretation is based on the understanding that the text is basically a citation of the Septuagint version of Malachi 3:1, whose messenger is referred to as Elijah in 3:23:

> Behold, I am sending my messenger
> to prepare the way before my face. . . .

> Lo, I will send you Elijah, the prophet,
> before the day of the Lord comes,
> the great and terrible day . . . (NAB).

There are some differences in the texts, of course,[12] but the crux of the matter is that the gospel tradition seems to have been adjusted so that the one whose way was to be prepared was no longer Yahweh, as Malachi would have it, but another, presumably, the Messiah. What prepared for this change in the text was said to be the existence of a popular legend in

---

[12] See R. Pesch, *Das Markusevangelium,* I 78.

contemporary Judaism which spoke of Elijah's return as precursor to the Messiah.

We have already seen, however, that there is no evidence
for such a tradition at the time of Jesus. If that is indeed the
imagery implied in the present text, then we must conclude
that it was a Christian innovation. But, having said as much,
we must not automatically see that pattern here. J. Fitzmyer,
in fact, has argued that although the context within the Gospels
is indeed messianic and hinges at least implicitly on an Elijah
model, the citation itself lacks any messianic reference, but
simply presents John as the messenger of Malachi whom God
sent before Jesus.[13]

On the other hand, it is important to consider the implications of the work of R. H. Gundry,[14] who has demonstrated
that the citation is in fact more than first meets the eye, and
has raised some serious questions in this regard. He was not
the first to describe the citation as a composite text, but he has
made it very clear that its basic, and therefore predominant,
component is not the Septuagint of Malachi 3:1, but that of
Exodus 23:20.[15] In fact, according to Gundry, Malachi 3:1 (in
its Hebrew form!) exerted only a "very slight influence" on
our text. Why then do we insist on giving so much weight to
the influence of Malachi in our interpretation? Two reasons
suggest themselves: first, the portrait of John that we have in
Mark's Gospel and second, closely related to that, the teaching of John that is summarized in Mark 1:7-8.

We do not wish to discount that influence in the latter stages
of the tradition as we find it for instance in Matthew. But, along
with the tradition, we ought to move slowly in accepting that
as the original meaning of the text. It is interesting to note that
Matthew himself seems to have found it necessary to do just
that, as is suggested in his hesitant and yet dramatic addition
of verse 14 to the discourse in chapter 11 of his Gospel: "And

---

[13] *Luke* I, 670–676.

[14] *The Use of the Old Testament in St. Matthew's Gospel* (Leiden: E. J. Brill,
1967) 11–12. The similarity of the two texts would seem to have invited
this combination of the two already in the Jewish tradition; see K. Stendahl, *The School of St. Matthew*, (Upsala: Gleerup, 1954) 47–54.

[15] "See, I am sending a messenger before you, to guard you on the
way, and bring you to the place I have prepared."

if you are willing to accept it, he is Elijah who is to come"
(RSV). The introductory phrase here suggests that there is a
difficulty in accepting this text as a reference to Elijah and John
in the Matthean community. Is this because of the heavenly
and "messianic" function of Elijah? For Luke this is not the
case; he has no intention of applying the Elijah model to the
Baptist, and the text does not force him to do so!

If that is so, then one may not simply ignore the existence
of the Exodus reference, especially since, in itself, it adds nothing to the Malachi text, while the opposite is not true. The notion of the messenger of Yahweh preparing the way is central
to both texts. The view which sees this in some way related
to the Messiah Jesus is dependent upon the supposed change
in the object of the messenger's activity from "Yahweh" to
"You," under the influence of Malachi. But if the Exodus text
is the basic one, that supposition is no longer necessary, for
the second-person form is already in that text. Who then, is
the "You" to whom it refers? In the Exodus reference the
"you" whose way is being prepared is Israel itself, certainly
not a bad referent in terms of the ministry of John! The implication that the "messenger" is then further specified as Elijah
is perhaps reason enough for this complex of texts to have been
applied to John, who, as we have seen, was already so likened
during his own ministry.

And yet there is more, for, in terms of legitimation, what
Malachi adds to the Exodus citation is not only the Elijah
model, but the very witness of the Prophets themselves. In
other words, this messenger, who comes on behalf of Yahweh,
has been attested by both Torah and Prophets! In this reading
of the text, therefore, it is not the Messiah who is being addressed, but Israel, whose way is being prepared by the messenger. If this is indeed the case, then the picture we have in
"Q" is that John's mission to Israel is presented as having
indeed been sanctioned by both Torah and Prophets.

What we have in this text, therefore, at the earliest level of
its redaction, and followed at least by Luke, is not an ordering
of John and Jesus in terms of their relationship to one another,
but an image of John as the one who is to prepare Israel for
the action of Yahweh in its midst. In fact it may have little to
do with Jesus at all except in so far as he was a disciple of John

among whom this tradition would have arisen. In this it serves as a middle ground in the developing saga of John and Elijah and would explain why it was that the equation of John and Elijah became such a problem in the Gospels.

Elijah and the Gospel of the Lord

Was John Elijah or was he not? If indeed there are such questions about John and Elijah in the early years of the Christian movement, how were they to be resolved? In the ordinary course of justifying a troubling ministry among the people, John had been likened to Elijah the Tishbite, a "troubler" of Israel from another time. Now his ministry was given a further divine sanction and spoken of in eschatological and perhaps even messianic terms. For the early Christians, this could be but the beginning of the discussion. We can see this in the Gospel of Mark, which introduces this image of Elijah and uses it to great advantage, ultimately giving it what is to become its specifically Christian modulation.

Mark begins his Gospel with the appearance of the Baptist in the desert, dressed in the garments of a prophet and proclaiming *(kerysson)* a "baptism of repentance for the forgiveness of sins" (Mark 1:4). In Mark, this is not a prophetic call to conversion, but a proclamation of the gospel that divine favor—forgiveness—is at hand.[16] The baptism that he proclaims is not his own; it is the one to be given only by the Stronger One who is to come after him.[17] This proclamation is, in turn, contrasted to his own practice of water baptism, which is but a shadow and prophetic preparation of the announced baptism in the Holy Spirit which is soon to be given. Note how Matthew (3:2) replaces this proclamation of forgiveness with

[16] There is a distinction in the narrative between the proclamation of John and his practice of baptism. Both verse 4 and verse 7 are introduced by the verb *keryssein* while his practice of water baptism is strikingly contrasted to the Spirit baptism of the future. I owe the basis of these remarks to E. Lohmeyer, *Das Evangelium des Markus*, 17th ed. (Göttingen: Vandenhoeck & Ruprecht, 1967) 12–19.

[17] Note how Matthew retains the verb *keryssein* but replaces this proclamation of forgiveness with the proclamation of the coming of the kingdom.

a call to conversion in the face of the coming kingdom. Yet at the same time, in 26:28, he connects the forgiveness of sin with the death of Christ, a notion that is notably absent in the Mark and Lukan parallels (Mark 14:24; Luke 22:20). In effect, the result is that Matthew has as much set a distinction between John and Jesus in this summary of John's preaching as he has made a parallel between them.[18] On the other hand, he does not differ in his overall presentation of the gospel proclamation in this matter.

Mark goes on to tell his readers that all the people, both the country folk of Judea and the city dwellers of Jerusalem, came out to the desert to accept John's baptism, confessing their sins as a prophetic sign of their readiness for the end-times. Thus is the Way of Israel prepared for the coming of the Lord. The messenger who was foretold in the Scripture has come!

But Mark goes further than that, for he has added to his citation of Exodus-Malachi, with its focus on the preparation of Israel, a quotation from Isaiah 40:3, so that the text now reads:

> "Behold, I send my messenger before thy face,
> who shall prepare thy way;
>
> 'the voice of one crying in the wilderness:
> Prepare the way of the Lord,
> make his paths straight' " (RSV).

As we have seen, this text from Isaiah is the same text which was used during John's ministry to describe the Baptist's work. In fact, the narrative which follows serves to illustrate the text and therefore show its fulfillment in the activity of the Baptist (vv. 4-11). With a slight adjustment, Mark is able to synchronize the two texts so that the focus is now precisely on the desert as the place of the eschatological preparation and the confes-

---

[18] It is difficult to agree with J. P. Meier ("John the Baptist in Matthew's Gospel," *Journal of Biblical Literature* 99 [1980] 388) and his criticism of J. Hughes ("John the Baptist: the Forerunner of God Himself," *Novum Testamentum* 14 [1972] 191-218) on this point. See also G. D. Kilpatrick (*The Origin of the Gospel according to St. Matthew*, London: Oxford University, 1946) as quoted in Meier, 389.

sion of sin together with a ritual cleansing as its mode. Furthermore, the coming of the messenger becomes a preparation for
the coming not of Yahweh, but of Jesus, who is here clearly
presented as "Lord," the Messiah and Son of God whose
Gospel the evangelist proclaims (Mark 1:1). Thus Mark is able
to situate John and Jesus in a relationship that would not only
be acceptable to his Christian readers but, at the same time,
service his own messianic Christology, which will be developed along those lines in the remainder of the Gospel. The
proclamation of the Gospel begins with the appearance of John,
whose own proclamation centers upon the forgiveness of sins
which will be brought about by the baptism in the Holy Spirit
given by the One Who Comes after him. Thus the eschatological prophet who in word and deed prepares Israel for the
Way of the Kyrios is in fact John who prepares the way of Jesus.

But that Way does not consist solely in his coming to earth.
The whole argument of Mark's Gospel is that the readers must
understand Jesus' messiahship in holistic terms so that they
might follow him along his way. Its creed is akin to that of
Romans 1:3-4, as chapter 12 of the Gospel makes clear. Jesus
becomes Messiah and Son of God only after his death. But already at the beginning of the story, his baptism by John stands
as a messianic anointing in preparation for his death.[19] And
so the "way of the Lord" for which John prepares Israel (and
the reader of the Gospel) consists in the suffering and death
of Jesus "for the forgiveness of sins" and culminates in his
own death, which, like that of the disciples, follows upon the
Way of the Cross.

Yet none of this is clear at the beginning of the narrative.
In fact, the full likeness of John to Elijah does not become clear
until chapter 9 of the Gospel, when Jesus answers the question of the disciples about "Elijah coming first." It is because
of this redactional positioning of the Elijah question and the
reflection of its content into other parts of the Gospel that the
reader can then understand that John is indeed Elijah, the one
to whom the Scriptures referred, who "came first." As a reader
of Mark's Gospel, Matthew was then able to use this insight

---

[19] This is the force of the scriptural background of the voice from the
open heavens in verse 11. See C. Kazmierski, *Jesus, the Son of God*, 53–71.

to develop the Elijah image he found in "Q" that was waiting to be further exploited.

Summary

The death and resurrection of Jesus had a profound effect on his own disciples' understanding of what he had taught them, and indeed of who he was and how he fit into the over-all plan of God for his people. Taking their lead from the patterns of study and celebration that were already in place during their time together with him, the early Christians turned to the Scriptures and to the dynamics already at work in the mission to Israel that they had shared. The development of a specifically Christian form of Davidic theology which centered upon the resurrection of Jesus as the fulfillment of all eschatological hope enabled them to situate John the Baptist in a new perspective vis-à-vis Jesus, who had now become their heavenly Lord and Messiah. Thus John the Baptist was to take on a new focus in the Christian perspective of things. This "prophet like Elijah" indeed was now seen to be the "Elijah who must come first" to prepare the Way of the Lord—in word, in deed, and in destiny.

6

The Stones of Abraham

We are quite fortunate in trying to understand John the Baptist, for the tradition of narratives and sayings which relate to his person and work is very rich and varied. We know full well that these traditions reflect not only the immediacy of his own situation, but also the developing challenges that his person provoked in the early days of the Church. We have already seen how complex that tradition is. What is so fascinating is that his own followers as well as the early Christians maintained the power of his presence precisely as a positive force within the ongoing life of the movement. Were they not, in this, remaining faithful to John?

Yet there is a text which might suggest otherwise. It is a text which we have not yet examined, a text which contains a prophetic judgment said to summarize the essence of the Baptist's teaching.

> You brood of vipers!
>
> Even now the axe is laid to the root of the tree.
> Every tree that is not fruitful will be cut down
> and thrown into the fire (NAB).

We must now, finally, examine this oracle and attempt to understand the situation in which it was pronounced and handed down in the early days of the Christian mission. To do that, however, we must first listen to words spoken by some of the earlier prophets and visionaries of Israel.

The Temple of the Lord

In one of the most dramatic moments in all of biblical literature, the prophet Ezekiel describes a vision he had, "sitting in (his) house on the fifth day of the sixth month of the sixth year, in the presence of the elders of Judah" (Ezek 8:1). The spirit lifted him up, he says, between earth and heaven and brought him, "in visions of God" to the holy city of Jerusalem. He had seen other visions of the city and its Temple, visions in which the abominations were so great that they would call down upon themselves the fury of the Lord. But now he is brought once again to the holy city. "And there (in the Temple)," he says, "I saw the glory of the God of Israel!" (v. 4).

As with Isaiah before him, the prophet is overwhelmed by the experience. He falls on his face, and cries out to God in a loud voice, "Alas, Lord God! will you utterly wipe out what remains of Israel?" (11:13 NAB). It had been a frightening vision, for, standing to the right of the Temple, Ezekiel had seen the cherubim with the four faces and four wings and the wheels beside each one. Burning coals were taken from beneath this throne of God, to be thrown over the holy city. "Then," he relates, in the most devastating revelation of all, "the glory of the LORD left the threshold of the temple . . ." (10:18 NAB)!

It was not long after the events of Pentecost, Luke tells us, that another holy man had a vision that to many in Israel was to be as threatening as was the vision of Ezekiel. "Stephen . . . filled with the Holy Spirit, looked to the sky above and saw the glory of God, and Jesus standing at God's right hand" (Acts 7:55 NAB).

Stephen had been chosen along with six others to serve the needs of the Hellenist Christians of Jerusalem,[1] whose

---

[1] The identity and position of the Hellenists and of the Seven have been the object of intensive debate for some time. See M. Simon, *Stephen and the Hellenists in the Primitive Church* (London: Longmans, Green, 1958); R. Pesch, "Hellenisten und Hebräer," *Biblische Zeitschrift* 23 (1979) 87–

"widows were being neglected in the daily distribution of food
. . ." (Acts 6:1 NAB).[2] In fact, however, he begins almost immediately to make his mark not as someone who waits on
tables, but as a "doer of wonders and signs" and a "speaker
of great wisdom and spirit."[3] As a result, it was not long until
a tense situation arose among the Greek-speaking Jews of the
city, who bring a charge of blasphemy against Stephen: "This
man never stops making statements against the holy place
and the law. We have heard him claim that Jesus the Nazorean
will destroy this place and change the customs which Moses
handed down to us" (6:13-14 NAB).[4] Chapter 7 of Acts is
devoted to the wonderfully crafted discourse in which Stephen
clarifies his stance in the presence of the Sanhedrin.[5] It becomes
the moment of confrontation which will ultimately seal the fate
of Stephen and the group which had gathered about him and
at the same time force the young Christian communities to
come to grips with the implications of their own developing
worldview.

92; E. Larsson, "Die Hellenisten und die Urgemeinde," *New Testament
Studies* 33 (1987) 205–225; and especially, M. Hengel, "Between Jesus and
Paul. The 'Hellenists,' The 'Seven,' and Stephen (Acts 6.1-15; 7.54–8.3),"
Between Jesus and Paul. Studies in the Earliest History of Christianity, (Philadel-
phia: Fortress, 1983) 1–29.

[2] See James M. Fennely, "The Jerusalem Community and Kashrut
Shatnes," *Society of Biblical of Literature 1983 Seminar Papers*, ed. Kent Harold
Richards (Chico: Scholars Press, 1983) 273–288, for a discussion on the
socioeconomic questions reflected in this text segment.

[3] B. Domagalski, "Waren die 'Sieben' (Apg 6,1-7) Diakone?" *Biblische
Zeitschrift* 26 (1982) 1–33.

[4] This is an indication of the somewhat conservative nature of these
Jews as a whole. In this view, Stephen and the Christian Hellenists would
stand out markedly from them. See Hengel, "Between Jesus and Paul,"
especially p. 18. For another position, see G. Baumbach, "Die Anfänge
der Kirchenwerdung im Urchristentum," *Kairos* 24 (1982) 17–30.

[5] For an exhaustive study of Stephen's speech see J. Kilgallen, *The
Stephen Speech: A Literary and Redactional Study of Acts 7:2-53*, (Rome: PIB,
1976) and E. Richard, *Acts 6:1–8:4: The Author's Method of Composition*,
Society of Biblical Literature Dissertation Series 41; Missoula: Scholars,
1978).

In our world of visions, however, Stephen does not stand alone. The Scriptures brought testimony to the fact that centuries before, Jeremiah had stood in this same place. "Stand at the gate of the house of the Lord," he had been told, "and there proclaim this message:

> Hear the word of the Lord,
> all you of Judah who enter these gates to worship the Lord! . . .
> Put not your trust in the deceitful words:
> 'This is the temple of the Lord! The temple of the Lord! The temple of the Lord!' . . .
> But here you are, putting your trust in deceitful words to your own loss!
> (Jer 7:2, 4, 8 NAB).

As if sharing in the very mission given to Jeremiah, Jesus too had stood among these same people who now had their eyes "fixed intently upon Stephen." The evangelist Mark relates how he had picked up on these very words of Jeremiah, and had hurled his own challenge at their feet. "Does not Scripture have it," he charged,

> " 'My house shall be called a house of prayer for all peoples'—?
> but you have turned it into a den of thieves!" (Mark 11:17 NAB).

Now it was Stephen who stood among them, making his answer to the same charges that had faced Jesus and Jeremiah before him. Surely the connection could not escape them.

In effect, within Luke's narrative, Stephen's speech is not a defense of his position, but a prophetic indictment of his contemporaries, made at the heart of their power structure. Stephen rehearses their history, stressing again and again their rejection of Moses and the Prophets. Now, Stephen asserts, their history has come full circle, this time once and for all. They who had ". . . received the law through the ministry of angels . . ." (NAB), had not observed it. The Scripture itself had repeatedly warned them. ". . . I will enter into judgment with you face to face," Ezekiel had promised (20:35 NAB). For Ezekiel, it was to be a new beginning, a rebirth of a people who would know the Lord . . . and be accepted as a pleasing odor to him (cf. 20:41, 42). But they had not listened. The words of the Prophets were fulfilled,

> "Thus says the Lord: If you disobey me, not living according to the law I placed before you and not listening to the words of my servants the prophets, whom I send you constantly though you do not obey them, I will treat this house like Shiloh, and make this the city which all the nations of the earth shall refer to when cursing another" (Jer 26:4-6 NAB).

What Stephen was telling them was that what to their ears was blashemy had been proclaimed by the Prophets of old. God had once again abandoned the Temple and the holy city and would now turn God's face to those who had seen God's glory and that of ". . . the Son of Man standing at his right hand" (7:56 NAB). "The Most High does not dwell in buildings made by human hands!" In a dramatic and emotion-filled fit of rage, those present drag Stephen outside the city and stone him to death.

In the ensuing violence, the Hellenist Christians at Jerusalem are scattered "throughout the countryside of Judea and Samaria" (8:1 NAB) and as far away as "Phoenicia, Cyprus and Antioch" (11:19 NAB). The scattering turns out to be a blessing in disguise, for it is in the work of these Hellenists that the door was to be opened to the acceptance of Samaritans into the Church. And soon the community at Antioch would begin to struggle with the question of whether and to what extent the Gentiles themselves could become a part of the community of the Messiah.[6]

This story of the Hellenist Christians in Acts is therefore an important one for understanding the spread of Christianity in its earliest years. But it is also important for understanding the growth of a certain ambiguity towards Judaism which arises in its very bowels. These were Jews from Jerusalem, whose working language was Greek and who, while remaining faithful to the traditions of their elders, some perhaps even to an extreme degree, were nevertheless, more than the rest, open

---

[6] See Raymond E. Brown and John P. Meier, *Antioch and Rome: New Testament Cradles of Catholic Christianity* (New York and Ramsey: Paulist, 1983) 6–8, 28–44.

to forces which would have threatened the seats of power. On the one hand, this would present new opportunities for the appropriation of the teachings of the Jesus faction and perhaps allow for its development within the parameters of the broad range of Jewish factions among them. But on the other, the murder of Stephen by members of the Sanhedrin would turn them away from Israel and lead them to conclude that the nation itself was forsaken, thus completing the final break with the ideological structures of the center.

> "Jerusalem, Jerusalem, killing the prophets and stoning those who are sent you! How often I would have gathered your children together as a hen gathers her brood under her wings, and you would not. Behold, your house is forsaken and desolate!" (Matt 23:37-38 RSV).

This theme of prophetic rejection is found in a number of places in the gospel tradition. Luke's use of it in his "defense" of the Stephen group is not unique, but rather illustrates a widespread cleavage which develops between the groups in their confrontations of mutual challenge and accusation. It becomes a kind of "theology of recrimination" which pervades the consciousness of a very significant portion of the early Jesus group. While its roots may lie deep within the prophetic tradition, its force within the Christian movement was reinforced by the experience of rejection faced by these early Hellenist followers of Jesus. Now they were to respond with their own form of counterjudgment and rejection.

"If any place will not receive you," they had been told, "and they refuse to hear you, shake its dust off your feet as a testimony against them" (Mark 6:11-12). The raising of that dust would cause a bitter taste to settle in their mouth for the violent rejection that seemed so often to face them. The rejection that Jesus had faced was now to be their lot as well. Stephen was but the next in a long line that stretched back to Jeremiah and even beyond. At any rate, it was not a large step for them to see John the Baptist in this same light, a prophet rejected by his people. It is not unreasonable to suggest, then, that such sentiments would find a firm footing within the gospel traditions which can be traced to these Hellenists, as they carried the Jerusalem gospel to the outreaches of their own country as well as to Syria and, as Luke suggests, "to the very ends of the earth."

The struggles of Paul and the dissidence of the community of the Beloved Disciple seem to stem in large measure from the insights developed within this movement. That is not to say that they were in any way unfaithful to the traditions of Jesus, or for that matter of the Jerusalem and Judeo-Christian Churches. Was not his own critique of the Temple and its ruling elite at the core of the tradition? Was it not, in fact, the ultimate cause of his downfall? Indeed the Gospels mark the charge that Jesus would destroy the Temple as "false witness," but if the parable of the Wicked Vinedressers is in any way authentic, he had certainly given his opponents ammunition for their attack. "What will the owner of the vineyard do? He will destroy the tenants, and give the vineyard to others!" (Mark 12:9 RSV). It is the pervasiveness of these traditions which would suggest, perhaps, that they were not such radical departures from the teaching of Jesus himself, and perhaps of John as well.

The End of Torah

It should not be surprising that such rejection often causes bitterness and even a lashing out at one's opponents, especially if those rejected have come announcing what was proclaimed to be gospel: the good news from God. Sometimes it is the only way to survival in a struggle for contending positions. "Deflection of criticism," it is often called, or, in a more scientific vein, "the condemnation of condemners."[7]

> "You brood of vipers!
> Who warned you to flee from the wrath to come? . . .
> Do not even begin to say to yourselves,
> 'We have Abraham as our father,'
> For I say to you, that God can raise up these very stones to be children of Abraham" (Matt 3:7, 8, 9).

[7] E. Pfuhl, *The Deviance Process*, 65–68.

What a harsh saying! In all the tradition we have of the teaching of John the Baptist, this one stands out by far as the most startling. In fact, it is the only one to take the form of such a radical and total condemnation of its audience. It is a teaching which is presented as a prophetic oracle in which the wrath of God is at issue, to be manifest in a judgment which is said to be sure, imminent, and utterly horrible. "Even now, the axe is already laid at the root of the tree. Every tree that is not fruitful will be cut down and thrown into the fire." It is the Day of the Lord that has come down upon them, a day of ". . . darkness and not light, gloom without any brightness" (Amos 5:20 NAB). Those who stand under this judgment are powerless to avert it.

How unlike what we have already seen of John's message;[8] yet, there is always the other side of the coin: the bad news of the gospel for those who do not accept the offer of grace. Such threats had been used before. "Woe to those who yearn for the day of the Lord!" (NAB), Amos had warned. It was to be, in the words of Zephaniah, "a day of wrath . . . a day of anguish and distress, a day of destruction and desolation, a day of darkness and gloom, a day of thick black clouds" (1:15 NAB). Nothing would be able to save those who stood under judgment on that day, "When in the fire of his jealousy all the earth shall be consumed. For he shall make an end, yes, a sudden end, of all who live on the earth" (NAB). Indeed, there was prophetic precedent for such language!

The text of this oracle, however, has been given a great burden to bear, for in the minds of most exegetes it stands as the singular example of the teaching of the historical John. It lacks, in their view, the Christological motivation that is said to mark the remainder of the Baptist tradition and serve as a pointer to the Christian manipulation of Baptist theology. Yet such a radical picture of his preaching is not even hinted at in the remainder of the Baptist tradition and would cause great difficulties in any explanation of the way in which the traditions about him have, in fact, developed. We must wonder, therefore, if this preaching of fiery doom with its vicious at-

---

[8] The position which is developed here was extensively argued in my article in *Biblica* 68 (1987) 22–40.

tack on the sincerity of his audience is indeed the teaching of John. Was it really this bad side of the gospel that John proclaimed? Or would these words, perhaps, find a better home in the circle of those Christian prophets influenced by the experience of Stephen and his group?

Both Matthew and Luke have provided somewhat different contexts for this teaching, but in each instance it is directed to people who had come out to hear John and, in fact, to accept baptism at his hands. This is one of the things that makes it such a difficult saying to deal with, for it implies a monstrous hypocrisy on the part of these people. Of course this may in fact have been the case, but one is constrained to tread a little more lightly here. In Matthew, the Baptist is castigating the Scribes and Pharisees who were the favorite opponents of the evangelist; but in Luke, it is the common people who come out in large numbers to John. These would seem to be a very unlikely target for such vitriolic abuse in that Gospel, for such it can honestly be termed. The evangelist is embarrassed and as he adapts the tradition of his source, must plead ignorance on the part of the crowd!

"Produce fruit which befits repentance!" he demands of them. But what is that fruit? It cannot lie in a return to Torah observance, as is often supposed, for they are told not even to consider the fact that they are Abraham's children. Recourse to ethnic privilege, even that based on the covenant, is to no avail. This is no longer the time for that, "for the axe is already laid to the root of the tree." This oracle is directed not to averting disaster; that is no longer possible. The judgment has already begun! This is an announcement of its impending arrival, and calls for them to produce a sign which recognizes that fact. The prophet is no longer concerned with the abuse of power, but with the source of power itself. At issue here is the means of salvation now that reliance on the media heretofore available to them as children of the covenant is no longer fruitful. To say that as sons of Abraham they have the means to escape the wrath to come marks them, in the eyes of the prophet, as a brood of vipers, for that is not the fruit of repentance that he seeks. The historic prerogative of Israel counts for nothing. What is called for now is a complete turning away from that which had historically assured Israel of salvation.

What is interesting, moreover, is that the text itself implies that the audience was indeed ready to heed the warning of the prophet. They would indeed "call upon Abraham" and repent as in the past. What they do not seem to accept, however, was the radical nature of the demands of this prophet. To turn away from the accepted means of salvation was beyond them. His solution was not one that was open to them, for within first-century Palestinian Jewish society, Temple and Torah remained central, even in the most radical of movements.

Many years ago, Rudolf Bultmann had suggested that the saying of John that we have here was actually a composite text, that is, an editorial joining together of disparate sayings that were originally attributed to Jesus, but in fact had been formed by the Church.[9] His was a view which was never really taken up by many exegetes, but which seems, in retrospect, to have much to be said for it. It may well be that while the gospel writers had received the text as a unit, Matthew, on his part, applied some of its elements to the situation of Jesus' ministry. But at the same time, the contexts which have been provided by the Gospels, and even "Q," are not required in any way by the saying itself. Is it not possible, therefore, and in light of the background we have suggested perhaps even probable, that we are dealing here with a saying which was originally independent of the limitations of its present contexts and therefore had entered the Baptist tradition, and indeed has shaped it from an entirely different perspective than that ordinarily presumed? In other words, its association with John the Baptist and with his practice of baptism may in fact be a secondary one. It is our contention that this is indeed the case, and that this saying, which the evangelists have used to heighten the eschatological character of the teaching of John, arose within the dynamic of the preaching of the early Christian Hellenists of the Stephen group that we have described above. The fruit of repentance to which it calls its hearers referred,

[9] See Matthew 7:19; 12:34; 23:33. Was this text originally associated with the Baptist? Of course the alternative would be that Matthew had chosen portions of the Baptist's sayings tradition and attributed them to Jesus, or that both said them!

not to the baptism of John, but to the Christian baptism which they offered. By adapting the text as the evangelists have, the Church was able to revitalize its tradition and use it to speak in a new time and a new place.

Conclusion

We have, in a sense, come to the end of our search. Yet, like John the Baptist, we have only prepared the way for a new and ongoing dialogue with the word of God that is enfleshed in the text. What we have found is a rich and diverse tradition about John the Baptist, a tradition that is present in every layer of the New Testament. It is a tradition which presents many challenges to professional exegetes and to ordinary readers of the Gospels as well, and certainly tells the lie to any who would produce a single or monolithic portrait of the Baptist. Having examined something of its complexity, we have attempted to ask questions that are respectful not only of the tradition but of its people and their place in its history. The answers we have heard suggest that a number of models were developed in the early days of the Church which reflect the people's attempts to remain true to John and to their growing understanding of his place in the history of God's people. Each of these has resulted in a portrait of the Baptist with its own parameters of meaning and probability, indeed some even seeming to be at a distance from the portraits of our faith. These patterns of interpretation that we have uncovered in our discussion can be summarized as follows.

(1) *John as Prophet and Evangelist.* This model is probably the oldest pattern of interpretation. It takes its inspiration from the text of Isaiah 40:3 (NAB):

In the desert prepare the way of the Lord!
Make straight in the wasteland a highway for our God!

This same Old Testament text served as a justification for the establishment of the Jewish community of Essenes at Qumran on the shores of the Dead Sea and had an influence on Jesus and the early Christian movement as well. We have argued that it reflects John's own understanding of his ministry and that adopted by his immediate followers. Accordingly, John is presented as one whose message is a joyous one, inviting his contemporaries to embrace his vision of the ever new and creative presence of God among them.

(2) *John as an Apocalyptic Preacher of Judgment.* This model is often said to represent the authentic John sometimes to the exclusion of all other possibilities. He is the ultimate ascetic preacher of hell and damnation who opposes the powerful and indeed any who might consider themselves among the pious in Israel, a kind of Savanarola of the first century. But, as we have pointed out, there are serious difficulties with this view. While it is altogether likely that there was a negative side to John's proclamation, we have argued that it must not dominate our understanding of the Baptist and his ministry. It is at most the flip side of the announcement of the good news of salvation that he proclaimed in the strains of the prophecies of the Second Isaiah. We have argued that the development of this portrait of the "Apocalyptic John" is the result of a crisis among a group of Hellenists within the early Christian movement who saw the rejection theme which lies at its base as a weapon in their own preaching of condemnation against their unbelieving brethren.

(3) *John as Elijah.* This pattern of interpretation has a number of different models. In its simplest form it is a straightforward comparison of John to Elijah, the prophetic troublemaker of Israel, and may reflect an image that was used by Jesus himself in his support of John. The early Christians were to take up this image and expand it with the help of the Book of Malachi and other Jewish traditions to present an understanding of John which was in line with their own recognition of Jesus as Messiah. John as Elijah is found primarily in Mat-

thew and Mark. Luke avoids the identification of John with Elijah and the Gospel of John clearly denies it (John 11:19-23).

(4) *John as Forerunner of the Messiah.* This is perhaps the favorite picture of the Baptist cherished by Christians today. It is a pattern that was probably developed in the early Church in response to the challenge presented by the Christian belief in the messiahship of Jesus to their actual memory of John and his relationship to Jesus. It is reflected primarily in the development of the Elijah model along lines not previously found in Jewish tradition.

(5) *John as Witness to the Messiah.* This is the predominant theme in the Gospel of John. It is first introduced in John 1:6-8 (NAB),

> "There was a man named John sent by God, who came as a witness to testify to the light, so that through him all men might believe—but only to testify to the light, for he himself was not the light."

and developed consistently in the remaining traditions. John is presented as subordinate to Jesus,

> ". . . he of whom I said, 'The one who comes after me ranks ahead of me, for he was before me' " (NAB).

His role is to testify to Jesus who is the "Lamb of God who takes away the sin of the world" (NAB).

While we may have been able to separate various portraits of John and discuss something of their origin and development within the life of the early Christian movement, we are led to recognize how beautifully they complement each other. Each one puts before us that feature of his mission which a new moment was to call forth. They continue to challenge, to balance and correct not only our view of John but of ourselves and of our place in the Church and world.

It has been our contention that it would be a mistake to view John as a sectarian in his time, or to separate him from his place in the heart of Christianity in our own. His interest was not in a separation from society but in a vision of reality which was rooted in the kingdom traditions of his people. His call to conversion was an invitation to all of Israel to take up its heritage rooted in their desert experience with the God whom they had heard, but who now seemed to be so silent. It was a call that was embroiled in controversy and dissent. That Jesus took up this vision and continued its proclamation in the villages of Galilee convinced many that their God had again visited them with a word of challenge and comfort. His life-giving sacrifice was seen as the completion of the gospel that many of them had sought in the waters of John's baptism. It was reason enough for the early Church to have clung to John in fascination and deep respect. The call to holiness which echoes across the pages of the sacred texts of our tradition is grounded in the reality of each of those portraits which have been left to us.

The struggles of our generation are certainly not those of the generation that John addressed. Nor are they the struggles of the early Church whose exegesis was to set the standard patterns of interpretation which allowed for the accommodation, reflection, and dialogue with his message in their own time. If the voice of the Baptist has been able to speak to generations across the centuries, it was because each of these generations had taken up his challenge and spent their time with him in the desert and had been able to clothe his message in an idiom that was their own.

The effectiveness of the Baptist's witness lay in his prophetic stance, in words of joy and consolation in the spirit of Isaiah that were to become a profound challenge to all those who would hear. Now it becomes a challenge to us as we seek to understand ourselves and our place in the order of God's creation.

And so our journey continues. But it is important that we respond knowing that it is a journey that is enlightened not only by the memory of the Baptist, but of his life in the Church as well. If we have been able in any measure to identify some of the early historical traditions, we recognize that they are nevertheless illumined by the splendor of the light that is cast on them by the person of the risen Jesus. John takes his place now standing with Jesus as the Elijah of Mount Tabor, bathed in that uncreated light of divinity about which the Eastern Fathers were so fond of speaking. The lens of their faith becomes the lens of our own. The invitation of the prophet thus frames the proclamation of the gospel in a new way and calls a new generation to respond to the challenge of new life that is to be found in the fire and water that is once again offered in the silence of the heart.

And that is the core. It is still an invitation to holiness, a joyful call to wholeness that is to be found in the kingdom of the Messiah. It is a call to meet God in the reality of our own existence, a call to justice-making and love, a call that offers to transform those who partake of its life and perhaps even in their own time undergo the fate of its prophets. Thus it is a call that leads to contemplation—and to Sabbath.

Bibliography

Annen, F. *Heil für die Heiden. Zur Bedeutung und Geschichte der Tradition von besessenen Gerasener (Mk 5,1-20 parr.).* Frankfurt am Main: Josef Knecht, 1976.

Baumbach, G. "Die Anfänge der Kirchenwerdung im Urchristentum." *Kairos* 24 (1982) 17–30.

Black, D. A. "The Text of Mark 6.20." *New Testament Studies* 34 (1988) 141–145.

Blank, J. "Die Sendung des Sohnes. Zur christologischen Bedeutung der Gleichnisses von den bosen Winzern." *Neues Testament und Kirche.* Ed. J. Gnilka. Freiburg: Herder, 1974, 11–41.

Boismard, M. E. "Constitue Fils de Dieu." *Revue Biblique* 60 (1953) 5–14.

Borg, M. *Conflict, Holiness and Politics in the Teachings of Jesus.* New York and Toronto: Edwin Mellen, 1984.

Braun, H. *Qumran und das Neue Testament.* Tübingen: J. C. B. Mohr (Paul Siebeck) 1966.

Brown, R. E. *The Birth of the Messiah.* Garden City: Doubleday, 1981.
_____. "Gospel Infancy Narrative Research from 1976 to 1986: Part II (Luke)." *Catholic Biblical Quarterly* 48 (1986) 660–680.
_____. *The Gospel According to John.* 2 vols. Garden City: Doubleday, 1966, 1970.

Brown, R. E., and J. P. Meier. *Antioch and Rome: New Testament Cradles of Catholic Christianity.* New York and Ramsey: Paulist, 1983.

Burkhill, T. A. "Sanhedrin." *Interpreter's Dictionary of the Bible* 4:214–218.

Cameron, P. S. *Violence and the Kingdom: The Interpretation of Matt 11:12.* Frankfurt am Main: Peter Lang, 1984.

Cameron, R. "What Have You Gone Out to See? Characterizations of John and Jesus in the Gospels." *Semeia* 49 (1990) 35–69.

Charlesworth, J. H. "The Historical Jesus in Light of Writings Contemporaneous with Him." *ANRW* II 25.1, 451–476.

Clifford, R. "The Hebrew Scriptures and the Theology of Creation." *Theological Studies* 46 (1985) 507–523.

Collins, J. J. "The Apocalyptic Technique: Setting and Function in the Book of Watchers." *Catholic Biblical Quarterly* 44 (1982) 91–111.

_____. *The Apocalyptic Imagination: An Introduction to the Jewish Matrix of Christianity.* New York: Crossroad, 1984.

Cross, F. M. *The Ancient Library of Qumran and Modern Biblical Studies.* Revised Edition; New York: Doubleday, 1961.

Danker, F. W. "Luke 16:16—An Opposition Logion." *Journal of Biblical Literature* 77 (1958) 231–243.

Dautzenberg, G. "Die Zeit des Evangeliums. Mk 1,1-15 und die Konzeption des Markusevangeliums." *Biblische Zeitschrift* 21 (1977) 219–234; 22 (1978) 76–91.

DeGeradon, B. "L'homme en l'image de Dieu. Approche nouvelle à la lumière de l'anthropologie de sens commun." *Nouvelle Revue Théologique* 80 (1958) 683–695.

Dodd, C. H. *The Apostolic Teaching and Its Developments.* London: Hodder Stoughton, 1936.

Domagalski, B. "Waren die 'Sieben' (Apg 6,1-7) Diakone?" *Biblische Zeitschrift* 26 (1982) 1–33.

Douglas, M. *Purity and Danger: An Analysis of Concepts of Taboo.* London: Routledge and Keegan Paul, 1966.

_____. *Natural Symbols: Explorations in Cosmology.* London: Penguin, 1973.

Dunn, J. D. G. "Sprit-and-Fire Baptism." *Novum Testamentum* 14 (1972) 81–92.

Ernst, J. *Johannes der Täufer Interpretation—Geschichte—Wirkungsgeschichte.* Berlin and New York: Walter de Gruyter, 1989.

Enslin, M. "John and Jesus." *Zeitschrift für die Neutestamentliche Wissenschaft* 66 (1975) 1–18.

Faierstein, M. "Why Do the Scribes Say that Elijah Must Come First?" *Journal of Biblical Literature* 100 (1981) 75–86.

Fennely, J. M. "The Jerusalem Community and Kashrut Shatnes." *SBL 1983 Seminar Papers,* ed. K. H. Richards. Chico: Scholars, 1983, 273–288.

Fitzmyer, J. *The Gospel According to Saint Luke.* Garden City: Doubleday, 1981.

_____. *Luke the Theologian: Aspects of his Teaching.* New York and Mahwah: Paulist, 1989.

_____. "More About Elijah Coming First." *Journal of Biblical Literature,* 104 (1985) 295–296.

Friedrich, G. "*Euangelion.*" *Theological Dictionary of the New Testament* 2: 229–234.

Gager, J. *Kingdom and Community: The Social World of Early Christianity.* Englewood Cliffs: Prentice Hall, 1975.

Gardner, R. B. *Jesus' Appraisal of John the Baptist: An Analysis of the Sayings of Jesus Concerning John the Baptist in the Synoptic Tradition.* Dissertation: Würzburg, 1973.

Golb, N. "The Problem of Origin and Identification of the Dead Sea Scrolls." *Proceedings of the American Philosophical Society* 124 (1980) 1–24.

_____. "Who Hid the Dead Sea Scrolls?" *Biblical Archaeologist* 48 (1985) 68–82.

Gottwald, N. K. *The Hebrew Bible: A Socio-Literary Introduction.* Philadelphia: Fortress, 1985.

Gundry, R. H. *The Use of the Old Testament in Matthew's Gospel.* Leiden: E. J. Brill, 1967.

Guttgemans, E. *Offene Fragen zur Formesgeschichte des Evangeliums. Eine methodische Skizze der Grundlagen der Form und Redaktionsgeschichte.* 2nd ed. Munich: Kaiser, 1971.

Haenchen, E. *Die Apostelgeschichte.* 6th ed. Göttingen: Vandenhoeck & Ruprecht, 1968.

Halliday, M. A. K. *Language as Social Semiotic: The Social Interpretation of Language and Meaning.* Baltimore: University Park, 1978.

Harrington, D. J. *The Maccabean Revolt: Anatomy of a Biblical Revolution.* Wilmington: Michael Glazier, 1988.

Hengel, M. *Between Jesus and Paul. Studies in the Earliest History of Christianity.* Philadelphia: Fortress, 1983.

Hoffmann, P. *Studien zur Theologie der Logienquelle.* Munster: Aschendorff, 1972.

Hollenback, P. "Social Aspects of John the Baptizer's Preaching Mission in the Context of Palestinian Judaism." *ANRW* II. 19.1 (1979) 850–875.

Holmberg, B. *Sociology and the New Testament: An Appraisal.* Philadelphia: Fortress, 1989.

Horsley, R. A. "Like One of the Prophets of Old: Two Types of Popular Prophets at the Time of Jesus." *Catholic Biblical Quarterly* 47 (1985) 453–463.

Horsley, R. A., and J. Hanson. *Bandits, Prophets and Messiahs: Popular Movements in the Time of Jesus.* Minneapolis: Winston, 1985.

Hudson, R. A. *Sociolinguistics*. Cambridge: Cambridge University Press, 1980.

Jeremias, J. "Elias." *Theological Dictionary of the New Testament* 2:934–941.

_____. *Die Sprache des Lukasevangeliums*. Göttingen: Vandenhoeck & Ruprecht, 1980.

_____. *Jerusalem in the Time of Jesus: An Investigation into Economic and Social Conditions during the New Testament Period*. Trans. F. H. and C. H. Cave. London: S.C.M., 1969.

Kazmierski, C. R. *Jesus the Son of God: A Study of the Markan Tradition and its Redaction by the Evangelist*. Würzburg: Echter, 1979.

_____. "The Stones of Abraham: John the Baptist and the End of Torah." *Biblica* 68 (1987) 22–40.

Keck, L. E. "The Spirit and the Dove." *New Testament Studies* 17 (1970) 41–67.

Kilgallen, J. *The Stephen Speech: A Literary and Redactional Study of Acts 7:2-53*. Rome: PIB, 1976.

Kraeling, C. *John the Baptist*. New York: Charles Scribners, 1951.

Larsson, E. "Die Hellenisten und die Urgemeinde." *New Testament Studies* 33 (1987) 205–225.

Leach, E. *Culture and Communication: The Logic by which Symbols are Connected*. Cambridge: Cambridge University Press, 1976.

Linnemann, E. "Tradition und Interpretation in Rom 1,3f." *Evangelische Theologie* 31 (1971) 264–276.

Lohmeyer, E. *Das Evangelium des Markus*. 17th ed. Göttingen: Vandenhoeck & Ruprecht, 1967.

Malina, B. J. "The Individual and the Community—Personality in the Social World of Early Christianity." *Biblical Theology Bulletin* 9 (1979) 126–138.

_____. *The New Testament World: Insights from Cultural Anthropolgy*. Atlanta: John Knox, 1981.

_____. "Jesus as Charismatic Leader?" *Biblical Theology Bulletin* 14 (1984) 55–62.

_____. "Religion in the World of Paul." *Biblical Theology Bulletin* 16 (1986) 92–101.

_____. *Christian Origins and Cultural Anthropology: Practical Models for Biblical Interpretation*. Atlanta: John Knox, 1986.

_____. "Christ and Time: Swiss or Mediterranean?" *Catholic Biblical Quarterly* 51 (1989) 1–31.

Malina, B. J., and J. H. Neyrey. *Calling Jesus Names: The Social Value of Labels in Matthew*. Sonoma: Polebridge, 1988.

Meier, J. P. "John the Baptist in Matthew's Gospel." *Journal of Biblical Literature* 99 (1980) 383–405.

Merklein, H. *Die Gottesherschaft als Handlungsprinzip. Untersuchung zur Ethik Jesu.* Würzburg: Echter, 1978.

Miller, R. J. "Elijah, John and Jesus in the Gospel of Luke." *New Testament Studies* 34 (1988) 611–622.

Mol, H. *Identity and the Sacred: A Sketch for a New Socio-Scientific Theory of Religion.* Oxford: Basil Blackwell, 1976.

Molin, G. "Elijahu der Prophet und sein Weiterleben in den Hoffnungen des Judentums und Christenheit." *Judaica* 8 (1952) 65–94.

Neusner, J. et al., eds. *Judaisms and their Messiahs at the Turn of the Christian Era.* Cambridge: Cambridge Univesity Press, 1987.

Perrin, N. *Rediscovering the Teaching of Jesus.* New York: Harper and Row, 1967.

Pesch, R. *Das Markusevangelium,* 2 vols. Freiburg, Basel, Wien: Herder, 1976, 1977.

_____. "Hellenisten und Hebräer." *Biblische Zeitschrift,* 23 (1979) 87–92.

Pfuhl, E. *The Deviance Process.* New York: Van Nostrand, 1980.

Reumann, J. "The Quest for the Historical Baptist." *Understanding the Sacred Text,* ed. J. Reuman. Valley Forge: Judson, 1972.

Richard, E. A. *Acts 6:1–8:4. The Author's Method of Composition.* Missoula: Scholars, 1978.

Rivkin, E. *What Crucified Jesus?* Nashville: Abingdon, 1984.

Robinson, J. A. T. "The Baptism of John and the Qumran Community: Testing an Hypothesis." *Harvard Theological Review* 50 (1957) 171–191.

Rotell J., ed. *The Works of Saint Augustine. A Translation for the 21st Century. Sermons I.* Brooklyn: New City, 1990.

Schenk, W. "Gefangenschaft und Tod des Täufers. Erwägungen zur Chronologie und ihren Konzequenzen." *New Testament Studies* 29 (1983) 453–483.

Schnackenburg, R. "Das Evangelium im Verständnis des Ältesten Evangelisten." *Orientierung an Jesus. Zur Theologie der Synoptiker,* eds. P. Hoffman et al. Freiburg: Herder, 1973, 309–324.

Scroggs, R. "The Earliest Christian Communities as Sectarian Movements." *Christianity and Other Greco-Roman Cults,* ed. J. Neusner. Leiden: E. J. Brill, 1975, 2:1–23.

Stendahl, K. *The School of St. Matthew.* Upsala: Gleerup, 1954.

Stuhlmacher, P. *Das paulinische Evangelium I. Vorgeschichte.* Göttingen: Vandenhoeck & Ruprecht, 1968.

Simon, M. *St. Stephen and the Hellenists in the Primitive Church.* London: Longmanns, Green, 1958.

Weber, H. R. *The Cross: Tradition and Interpretation.* London: S.P.C.K., 1979.
Weber, M. *Economy and Society,* trans. G. Roth and C. Wittich. Berkley: University of California, 1968.
Wink, W. *John the Baptist in the Gospel Tradition.* Cambridge: Cambridge University Press, 1968.
Zerwick, M. *Biblical Greek.* Rome: PIB, 1964.